Model-Based
Image Matching
Using Location

ACM Distinguished Dissertations

1982

Abstraction Mechanisms and Language Design,
by Paul N. Hilfinger

*Formal Specification of Interactive Graphics
Programming Languages,* by William R. Mallgren

Algorithmic Program Debugging,
by Ehud Y. Shapiro

1983

The Measurement of Visual Motion,
by Ellen Catherine Hildreth

Synthesis of Digital Designs from Recursion Equations,
by Stephen D. Johnson

1984

*Analytic Methods in the Analysis and Design
of Number-Theoretic Algorithms,* by Eric Bach

Model-Based Image Matching Using Location,
by Henry S. Baird

A Geometric Investigation of Reach,
by James U. Korein

Model-Based
Image Matching
Using Location

Henry S. Baird

The MIT Press
Cambridge, Massachusetts
London, England

This book was printed and bound in the United States of America.

Publisher's note: This format is intended to reduce the cost of publishing certain works in book form and to shorten the gap between editorial preparation and final publication. Detailed editing and composition have been avoided by photographing the text of this book directly from the author's typescript or word-processor output.

Dissertation submitted in October 1984 to the Department of Electrical Engineering and Computer Science, Princeton University, in partial fulfillment of the requirements for the degree of Doctor of Philosophy.

All editing, composition, and drafting were performed by the author using the UNIX 8th Edition tools ped, grap, pic, tbl, eqn, and troff, and printed on an APS-5 phototypesetter. (UNIX is a Trademark of AT&T Bell Laboratories.)

Library of Congress Cataloging in Publication Data

Baird, Henry S.
     Model-based image matching using location.

     (ACM distinguished dissertations)
     Thesis (Ph. D.)--Princeton University, 1984.
     Bibliography: p.
     Includes index.
     1. Pattern recognition systems. 2. Image processing
--Digital techniques. I. Title. II. Series.
TK7882.P3B35 1985   001.53'4   85-243
ISBN 0-262-02220-6

T O

H. Clark Maziuk

Of the terrible doubt of appearances,
Of the uncertainty after all, that we may be deluded,
That may-be reliance and hope are but speculations after all, ...
To me these and the like of these are curiously answer'd by my lovers, my
dear friends,
When he whom I love travels with me or sits a long while holding me by
the hand,
When the subtle air, the impalpable, the sense that words and reason hold
not, surround us and pervade us,
Then I am charged with untold and untellable wisdom, I am silent, I
require nothing further ....

Walt Whitman, *Calamus*

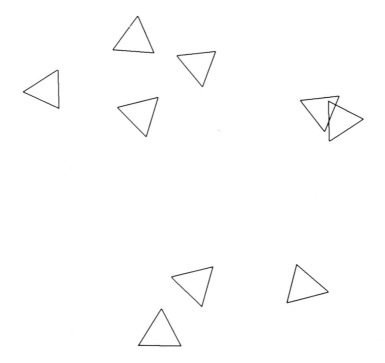

Frontispiece A. A model pattern, showing noise constraints.

Frontispiece B. A distorted instance of the model pattern.

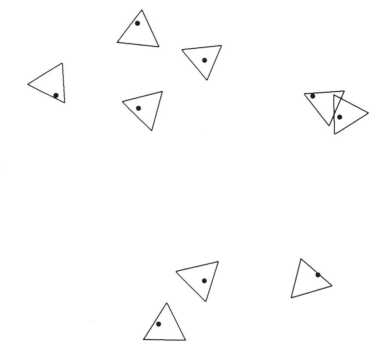

Frontispiece C. A successful match of instance to model.

Table of Contents

Table of Contents

Table of Contents

List of Illustrations

List of Illustrations

Series Foreword

This book is being published by The MIT Press as an outgrowth of the annual contest for the best doctoral dissertation in computer-related science and engineering. The contest was initiated in 1982 and is co-sponsored by ACM and The MIT Press.

The Distinguished Doctoral Dissertation Series has been created to recognize that some of the theses considered in the final round of selecting a contest winner also deserve publication. In the judgment of the ACM selection committee and The MIT Press, this thesis is of such high quality that it deserves special recognition in this new series.

Dr. Henry S. Baird wrote his thesis on "Model-Based Image Matching Using Location" at Princeton University. The thesis work was supervised by Professor Kenneth Steiglitz and was submitted to the 1984 competition. The Doctoral Dissertation Award Committee of the ACM recommended the publication of this thesis because it presents an elegant solution to the problem of matching a known "model" shape with an observed image of it. The assumption is that by translating, rotating, and scaling, one can match features found in the image with features of the model. Each feature is observed with some location error whose worst-case bounds are known. The thesis shows that this problem can be recast as the solution of a series of sets of linear inequalities, and so can be attacked using the Simplex and Soviet ellipsoid algorithms, among others. Surprisingly, the ellipsoid method runs substantially faster than Simplex for this problem. In addition, the method is shown to run in time linearly proportional to the number of features (for objects of reasonable complexity).

The committee found the statement and solution of the problem to be both elegant and relevant. The thesis is an excellent example of the interplay of theory and practice.

Charles L. Bradshaw

Chairman, Awards Committee
ACM

Preface

This work deals with the computer vision task of recognizing rigid patterns in the plane which have undergone unknown distortions. We view a pattern as a set of "locally-defined" features: that is, each can be located, independently of the rest, by examining small regions of the image.

Given a model pattern and an image, the goals of recognition are to match each image feature with the corresponding model feature, and to locate the overall instance of the model within the image. Finding such a "global" matching can be difficult, and provably near-linear-time algorithms to do so are rare.

Distortions studied include arbitrary translation, rotation, and scaling, and bounded location error ("noise"). Many prior workers have restricted attention to translation and small changes in rotation and scale. We permit noise bounds to be specified as arbitrary convex polygons about each model feature location.

We show that efficient recognition is possible even when only the location of features is known. A pruned tree-search method is developed which makes use of the Soviet ellipsoid algorithm for testing feasibility of systems of linear constraints. We give a general analysis of the geometry of constraints on distortions which are consistent with arbitrary matchings. The expected number of feasible partial matchings examined to find m successful matchings is proven to be $O(mn)$, where n is the number of pattern features. An interesting blend of theoretical analysis and practical implementation shows that the algorithm has an overall expected runtime that is theoretically asymptotically quadratic in n, but practically linear for patterns with fewer than 100 features.

These results hold for a class of random patterns, under moderate noise likely to occur in practice, and assuming there are no spurious or missing feature points in the image. If spurious or missing features occur, the algorithm's asymptotic runtime will worsen.

The approach extends directly to 3D patterns and more general affine distortions, at generally higher asymptotic costs. Although we have exploited only *location* of features, other properties such as orientation, size, order along boundaries, and semantic labels, can be easily used within the same framework of pruned search, for improved results.

Acknowledgments

To Professor Ken Steiglitz I owe many debts of gratitude, for reaching out to share my interest in the subject, helping considerably to focus and sharpen the topic, and contributing important insights to the finished work. I have found him to be a man of uncommon, even rigorous, integrity. His accessibility, candor, and irreverence steadied me through the months.

Theo Pavlidis was my stimulating and friendly first advisor at Princeton, and has remained an important guide. I am pleased that David Dobkin, whose courses in computational geometry and graphics I have enjoyed, agreed to serve on the committee.

During this long enterprise, many encouraging voices lifted my spirits. Leon Barnhart, Peter Aupperle, Avi Wigderson, Karl Lieberherr, Dick Ludwig, John Roberts, Bill Kirby, Paul Shupack, and Clark Maziuk have shown particular tact and kindness.

During this time I had the good fortune to befriend Leon Barnhart, also a tenacious PhD candidate, but in Philosophy: we swapped weekly dispatches of advances and retreats, and shared larger, personal strategies. He died suddenly, in February of this year, his work uncompleted. I would like my dissertation to serve, however imperfectly, as a memorial to his high ambitions.

Without the generous support of RCA Laboratories, my graduate study at Princeton would have been impracticable. I would like to thank particularly Al Korenjak, Fred Teger, and Art Kaiman for their support of my interest in machine vision for robotics. I am glad also to have justified the risk taken, years ago now, by Bede Liu and Bruce Arden of Princeton University's Department of Electrical Engineering and Computer Science, along with Edward Edenfield and Theodore Ziolkowski of the Graduate School, in approving a proposal for part-time study.

This work was supported in part by National Science Foundation grant ECS-8120037, U. S. Army Research Office grant DAAG29-82-K-0095, DARPA grant N0014-82-K-0549, and Office of Naval Research grant N0014-83-K-0275. Final editing and phototypesetting were done using the facilities of AT&T Bell Laboratories, Murray Hill, NJ.

Model-Based
Image Matching
Using Location

CHAPTER 1.

Introduction

We wish to recognize, in a planar image, an instance of a known model pattern. A pattern is simply a set of "locally-defined" features, each of which can be located independently of the rest by examining small regions of the image. The image may have been distorted by arbitrary translation, rotation, and/or scaling. In addition, each pattern feature's location may have moved a bit, within known worst-case bounds.

The recognition task includes both locating the overall pattern and identifying each of its features. Location is achieved by finding a geometrical "registration" function that does a good job of superimposing the instance and the model. Identifying the features requires matching each model feature with the corresponding instance feature.

1.1. Motivation

Our motivation for choosing this problem is rooted in a widely-accepted paradigm for computer vision [28] that distinguishes four stages of image processing: restoration (cleaning up the image), segmentation (partitioning into significant regions), description (extracting local features and relations among them), and model matching. Model matching involves recognizing patterns of features within an image description, guided by *a priori* models.

We will focus on model matching, and will assume that the earlier stages have been accomplished by some means. It oftens happens that "global" scene understanding, having been deferred during earlier stages, is first attempted at this stage. Many researchers have pointed out a need for demonstrably low-order polynomial algorithms in this area.

Much prior work on model matching has exploited non-geometric feature properties, in the form of semantic labels or order relations (*e.g.* along a boundary) [3 & 4]. We feel that geometric constraints have yet to be systematically exploited. To explore how geometric information can guide model matching, we have chosen to focus first on the uses of *location* alone. Thus, we abstract features as unlabeled points in the image plane.

1.2. Strengths of the Approach

An important aspect of the approach is that we seek to match instance features to the model features, in addition to finding a good registration. In general, knowing a good registration does not make it easy to find a good matching[1]. A matching cannot be found directly by use of transforms that do not preserve locality, such as Fourier coefficients and moments of area or boundary.

If matching fails, our method can report the most complete partial match found, and thus be used to isolate the missing or mislocated feature.

There are many methods, algorithmic [30] and optical, for registering images that are mistranslated, but relatively few cope with scale differences, and fewer still cope with arbitrary misrotations. Even optical processing is weak when faced with large rotations. We will cope with all three, and our approach generalizes to arbitrary non-singular affine distortions, as well as to patterns in higher dimensions than two.

We will accept constraints on matching error in the form of worst-case, pointwise, geometrical bounds. For each feature, the constraints may be specified as a convex polygon enclosing the feature point. This choice is partly motivated by

---

[1] Consider what happens when "best" is characterized by a minimum sum of pointwise errors; then, given a registration, the problem of finding a "best" matching can be transformed (in $O(n^2)$ time) into an instance of the Assignment (bipartite maximum weighted matching) problem, for which the best known algorithm is the Hungarian method, running in $O(n^3)$ time, where n is the number of feature points.

technical considerations which will become clear later. It is clear at once, however, that this offers certain advantages in practice. For example, it is a general and flexible representation, and gives a user broad latitude to model noise in ways most appropriate for each feature and feature extraction method. This contrasts with many earlier approaches using a noise bound that is identical for all features, or a global measure of noise that is insensitive to the error of an individual feature.

As we will see, the proposed method can exploit geometrical properties other than simple location, such as size and orientation of features, or prior knowledge of geometrical constraints, such as bounded scale. Also, the method can be readily adapted to exploit ancillary properties such as semantic labels and order relations, to improve our basic results.

The method can be extended to cope with arbitrary affine transformations of patterns in higher-dimensioned spaces, with the penalty, in general, of worse asymptotic runtimes.

1.3. An Important Limitation

We will concentrate on the special case where there are no spurious or missing feature points — that is, a matching succeeds only when it pairs *all* model points with *all* instance points.

This is an important restriction in practice, since it requires that (i) the object of interest is wholly in the field of view, (ii) it is not occluded by other parts, (iii) the image can be perfectly segmented, (iv) the object can be isolated from other shapes in the image, and (v) the feature extractor always finds the correct local features. Few scenes and few image analysis systems meet these requirements.

However, in the controlled world of industrial robot vision, they are occasionally met. Also, some feature-extractors are robust in this way: for example, the split-and-merge algorithm of Pavlidis and Horowitz for approximating boundaries by polygons [10] gives the same number of breakpoints over a wide range of digitizing resolutions and error bounds.

While focussing on this special case, we have looked for opportunities to extend our approach to more general cases. After the main results, we will describe the behavior of the algorithm when spurious and/or missing points occur. For only a few missing points, the algorithm should degrade gracefully. For many spurious points, we can suggest modifications that will, on average, reduce the growth in runtime.

1.4. An Unusual Feature

An unusual feature of our work is the use of the Soviet ellipsoid algorithm. This attracted wide attention in 1979 when it was used by Khachian to prove that linear programming was polynomial-time in the worst-case. However, early hopes that the method might lead to practical codes for linear programming have faded. We use the ellipsoid method to test for feasibility of systems of linear inequalities, for which it is particularly efficient. Recently, the Ellipsoid algorithm has been observed to be robust, numerically stable, and competitive among general nonlinear and geometric programming algorithms [29]. The application we propose for the Soviet ellipsoid algorithm is one of few known for which it is practically efficient and competitive with the Simplex algorithm.

CHAPTER 2.

Task Abstraction

In this chapter we define the model matching task precisely, with particular attention to a flexible representation for constraints on pointwise noise.

2.1. Point patterns

Define the *model* and *instance* point sets P and Q to be finite ordered subsets of points in the plane. $|P| = |Q| = n$.

The model is an *a priori* prototype pattern, extracted from a database or inferred from a training set. The instance is suspected to be a noisy, misregistered copy of the model. Any work to precondition the model or precompute its properties for use in recognition, we will consider to be a one-time expense, and not count towards asymptotic results.

2.2. Matchings

A *(partial) matching M* of *size k* is a one-to-one mapping from a subset of P of size k into Q; a *total matching* is a matching of size n, and so is a bijection from P onto Q. Using a matching, one can immediately identify features in the instance Q with known reference features in the model P. A matching of size k is written:

$$m_1 \ m_2 \ ... \ m_k$$

and is read: $\mathbf{q}_{m_1}$ is matched to $\mathbf{p}_1$, $\mathbf{q}_{m_2}$ is matched to $\mathbf{p}_2$, etc.[2] In the absence of constraints on feasible matchings, there are $n!$ distinct total matchings. An arbitrary matching may of course be geometrically absurd.

---

[2] Not all partial matchings of size $k < n$ can be expressed this way: we assume an order on the points of P, and match only the first k in this order. More on this later, in Section 4.1.

2.3. Registrations

A *registration* **R** is a one-to-one mapping from the Euclidean plane R^2 onto itself, consisting of a composition of translation, rotation, and positive (non-zero) scaling. It represents one choice of a "rigid" transformation superimposing the instance Q upon the model P.

Registrations can be represented in two useful ways, both being parameterizations with four independent variables. Conversion between the two forms is straightforward.

2.3.1. Trigonometric parameterization

The four real parameters:

$$< r_x, r_y, s, \theta > \qquad (s>0)$$

specify a registration **R** which acts on a point $\mathbf{p} = \begin{pmatrix} p_x \\ p_y \end{pmatrix}$ as follows:

$$\mathbf{R(p)} \equiv \begin{pmatrix} r_x \\ r_y \end{pmatrix} + s * \begin{pmatrix} \cos \theta & -\sin \theta \\ \sin \theta & \cos \theta \end{pmatrix} \begin{pmatrix} p_x \\ p_y \end{pmatrix} .$$

This is an intuitive representation: r_x and r_y are translation offsets, s is a scale factor, and θ is a rotation angle about the origin. (Note the obvious fact that $\mathbf{R(p)}$ is not linear in the parameter θ.)

2.3.2. Affine parameterization

The four real parameters:

$$< r_x, r_y, r_1, r_2 > \qquad (r_1, r_2 \text{ not both } 0)$$

specify registration **R** acting as follows:

$$\mathbf{R(p)} \equiv \begin{pmatrix} r_x \\ r_y \end{pmatrix} + \begin{pmatrix} r_1 & -r_2 \\ r_2 & r_1 \end{pmatrix} \begin{pmatrix} p_x \\ p_y \end{pmatrix} .$$

The matrix performs a combined scaling and rotation that is equivalent to the trigonometric form when $r_1 = s \cos \theta$ and $r_2 = s \sin \theta$. Written this way, the registration is linear in all four parameters — a property which can be exploited in the context of point-set matching, as we will see.

2.4. Pointwise Noise

Given a matching M and a registration $\mathbf{R}$, the location error vector they imply for point $\mathbf{p}_i$ is

$$\epsilon_i \equiv \mathbf{R}(M(\mathbf{p}_i)) - \mathbf{p}_i \qquad (2\text{-}1)$$

(note that we choose to measure errors in the model's scale). We adopt the view that this vector is due to noise in image acquisition or imprecision in feature extraction, and we call ϵ_i the *noise vector* of feature point $\mathbf{p}_i$, and call $\mathbf{R}(M(\mathbf{p}_i))$ the *noisy image* of $\mathbf{p}_i$ under M and $\mathbf{R}$.

2.5. Noise Constraints

We accept, along with the model P, worst-case constraints on pointwise noise, in the form of convex polygons in the plane (see Figure 2-1). That is, for $\mathbf{R}$ and M to satisfy the constraints, each model point $\mathbf{p}_i$'s noisy image $\mathbf{R}(M(\mathbf{p}_i))$ must lie within a region in the plane (containing $\mathbf{p}_i$), bounded by $j = 1,...,l_i$ straight sides each of which is defined by a linear inequality constraint of the form

$$\mathbf{u}_{ij}' \epsilon_i \leqslant d_{ij} \qquad (2\text{-}2)$$

where $\mathbf{u}_{ij}$ is a unit vector perpendicular to the side, d_{ij} is the closest distance of $\mathbf{p}_i$ to the side, and $'$ denotes scalar product (see Figure 2-2). Formally, a single constraint may be written $< \mathbf{u}_{ij}, d_{ij} >$, with the meaning of (2-2). The full set of constraints for $\mathbf{p}_i$ may be written $< \mathbf{U}_i, \mathbf{d}_i >$, where $\mathbf{U}_i$ is a $l_i \times 2$ matrix and $\mathbf{d}_i$ is a l_i vector; this implies the system of l_i simultaneous constraints:

$$\mathbf{U}_i \epsilon_i \leqslant \mathbf{d}_i$$

Also, we require that each polygon has no more than a small fixed number of sides, say l_{max}. This assumption helps establish reasonable asymptotic bounds.

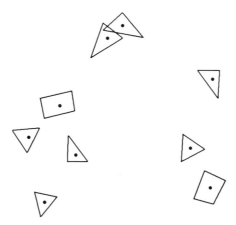

Figure 2-1.   A model specified as a set of noise polygons.

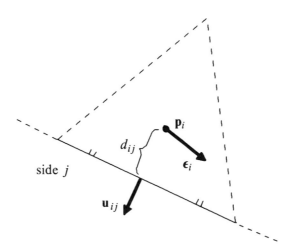

Figure 2-2.   Formal model of a noise constraint.

Many methods for feature extraction can provide worst-case bounds on the location error of features, and the class of polygons with a small number of sides is rich enough to provide good approximations for these in many cases. The location error of estimates of centroids and other features of discrete binary images has been studied by Hill [21] and Bolles & Cain [20]. There may be a need in practice for various shapes of noise envelopes: for example, a boundary-segmenting feature extractor may locate an obtuse corner more precisely in a direction normal to the boundary than along it, so that a noise polygon narrow normal to the boundary and wide along it is appropriate.

2.6. Feasible Matchings

Given a set of noise constraints for model P, we call a k-matching M *feasible* if there exists some registration $\mathbf{R}$ such that all pointwise location errors satisfy the constraints:

$$\mathbf{U}_i \, \epsilon_i \;\leqslant\; \mathbf{d}_i \qquad \text{for all } i = 1,...,k \;\; .$$

2.7. Abstract Planar Point-Matching Problem

We can now state our problem succinctly:

Given a pair of point sets P and Q $(|\mathrm{P}| = |\mathrm{Q}| = n)$, with noise constraints $\{ <\mathbf{U}_i, \, \mathbf{d}_i > \}_{i=1,...,n}$,

find all total feasible matchings M (and for each a registration $\mathbf{R}$, providing an explicit geometrical match).

CHAPTER 3.

Prior Approaches

Some prior workers have assumed, as we will, that there are no spurious or missing points (that is, $|P| = |Q|$, and all points are expected to match). Simon *et. al.* [11] compute all pairwise distances within the model and instance, and then use a comparison of sorted lists of these to constrain matchings. Experimental results using a relaxation method were reported. Seidl [13] measures similarity of point patterns, rather than seeking an explicit matching, using nearest neighbor relations. None of these papers gives asymptotic analysis of its algorithm.

Zahn [12] matches by comparing minimal spanning trees, without bounding the effects of noise. His algorithm apparently runs in $O(n^3)$ expected time.

Other workers allow spurious and/or missing points in the instance, as follows.

Price & Reddy [14], in a complex "symbolic" matching and registration system using ten properties of features including location, cope with translation and scale and, to a lesser extent, rotation misregistration. $O(n^2)$ pairwise match "ratings" are computed, and high ratings are heuristically confirmed.

Davis [38] finds approximate matches (together with registrations) of pieces of shapes (simple closed polygons) to pieces of larger shapes. Mis-registration includes translation, rotation, and a range of scale changes. First, figures of merit are assigned to pairwise-matched angles; then, a relaxation method is used to prune matchings. The method is robust, but "it is difficult to develop any useful absolute model for the complexity."

Barrow *et. al.* [15], seeking a "parametric correspondence" (more general than our registrations) between patterns composed of curve fragments and wire models as well as points, propose a "chamfer-matching" (hill-climbing) method in which each relaxation step requires time linear in the size of the model pattern. No asymptotic analysis of runtime is given. It is robust when the initial correspondence is close.

Kahl *et. al.* [8] restrict misregistrations to translation and small (10 degree) rotation. The algorithm apparently runs in $O(n^4)$ time. It is vulnerable to noise exceeding an *a priori* tolerance, but it is remarkably immune to spurious and missing point effects.

Ranade & Rosenfeld [16] restrict misregistrations to translation. Each matching of size 1 is rated by its effect on other points, and by a process of relaxation, a total matching is converged to. Experiments with uniform noise bounds are described. The method seems robust under some 'non-rigid' distortions, and runs in $O(n^4)$ time.

Tropf [17] uses a small set of semantic labels in addition to location. He explores a tree of partial matchings, pruning heuristically according to an *a priori* "similarity estimate". No asymptotic analysis is given.

Lavine *et. al.* [7] seek to recognize point patterns without finding an explicit matching. Misregistrations are restricted to translation and rotation. Like Simon they analyze sequences of interpoint distances, but in addition prove the correctness of their algorithm under a plausible noise model. No asymptotic analysis is given.

Ballard [23] has generalized the Hough transform to recognize and locate non-analytic shapes. A feature (in "image space") is mapped into a locus of possible registrations in the dual "parameter space." The parameter space is tiled and represented by an array of counters. Each feature point "votes" for registrations by incrementing counters in its dual locus. A global maximum count identifies a best registration. The method is efficient when feature properties include orientation and/or size as well as location. Managing noise is complicated by the discrete nature of the tiling.

Gennery [24] searches for a matching between sets of features of the same type. Error distribution is assumed Gaussian. Partial matchings imply a best (least-squares) registration whose Bayesian probability (computed using all features) is used to prune a breadth-first search tree using an *a priori* threshold. No asymptotic analysis is given.

Chazelle [39] has investigated an interesting related problem where the patterns are polygons: determine whether an n-gon can be moved to fit into an m-gon, if translations and/or rotations are allowed. If the stationary polygon is convex, he gives a worst-case $O(nm^2)$ algorithm. If only translations are allowed, he gives an $O(n+m)$ algorithm.

To summarize, only a few prior workers have attempted to find a matching in addition to a registration. Of those who have, only a few have coped with general similarity registrations. Of these, only one gives an analysis of asymptotic complexity, and this is $O(n^3)$ expected time.

By contrast, we will describe a method which finds a matching as well as a similarity transformation, in $O(n^2)$ time for "average" patterns under "moderate" non-zero noise, when there are neither missing nor spurious points. Furthermore, for small patterns ($<$ 100 points), performance should appear linear in n, since non-linear terms contribute less than 5% to runtimes, on average.

Figure 3-1 summarizes this review of prior work, and comparison with our results.

Researcher	Matching	Registration			Permits $|P| \neq |Q|$	Asymptotic runtime
		trans	rot'n	scale		
Simon 72	√	√	√	√	✕	?
Zahn 74	√	√	√	√	✕	n^3? e.c.
Seidl 74	✕	√	√	√	✕	?
Barrow 77	✕	√	√	√	√	?
Price 79	√	√	Δ	√	√	n^3? w.c.
Davis 79	√	√	√	Δ	√	?
Kahl 80	✕	√	Δ	✕	√	n^4 w.c.
Ranade 80	√	√	✕	✕	√	n^4 w.c.
Tropf 80	√	√	√	√	√	?
Lavine 81	✕	√	√	✕	√	?
Ballard 81	✕	√	√	√	√	n^4 w.c.
Gennery 81	√	√	√	√	✕	?
Chazelle 83	✕	√	√	✕	√	n^3 w.c.
Baird 84	√	√	√	√	✕	n^2 e.c.

Legend: √ — yes, has this feature
✕ — not this feature
Δ — yes, over small range
w.c. — worst-case
e.c. — expected-case

Figure 3-1. Summary of approaches to planar point-matching.

CHAPTER 4.

A Linear Programming Approach

Our approach to solving the planar point-matching problem is motivated by the observation that in the conditions for feasibility of k-matching M,

$$\mathbf{U}_i \, \boldsymbol{\epsilon}_i \; \leqslant \; \mathbf{d}_i \qquad i = 1, \cdots, k \quad ,$$

or, in more detail,

$$\mathbf{U}_i \, (\, \mathbf{R}(M(\mathbf{p}_i)) - \mathbf{p}_i \,) \; \leqslant \; \mathbf{d}_i \qquad i = 1, \cdots, k \quad ,$$

the $\mathbf{U}_i$, $\mathbf{d}_i$, $\mathbf{p}_i$, and $M(\mathbf{p}_i)$ are all known, so the conditions can be viewed as a system of $\sum_{i=1}^{k} l_i$ simultaneous inequality constraints on the unknown parameters of $\mathbf{R}$.

If we use the affine parameterization of registrations, this system is linear[1] in the parameters $< r_x, r_y, r_1, r_2 >$ (see Figure 4-1). Thus a matching M specifies a system of linear inequality constraints on $\mathbf{R}$ (see Figures 4-2 and 4-3). Testing the feasibility of systems of linear inequalities is a well-studied problem for which efficient algorithms exist: for example, the Simplex algorithm, the Soviet Ellipsoid algorithm, and Megiddo's algorithm [35,36].

4.1. Pruned Search

Our strategy is to use one of these feasibility-testing algorithms to prune a systematic search of matchings. Given model P with its noise polygons, choose a *comparison order* on the $\mathbf{p}_i$ which will remain fixed during matching, say: $\mathbf{p}_1 \, \mathbf{p}_2 \, \cdots \, \mathbf{p}_n .$[2] The instance Q's points are presented, of course, in an arbitrary

---

[1] The derivation of this is given later, in Section 5.3.2.

[2] As we will see, this choice affects runtimes. But, fixing a comparison order does not eliminate any matchings from consideration as long as no instance points are missing .

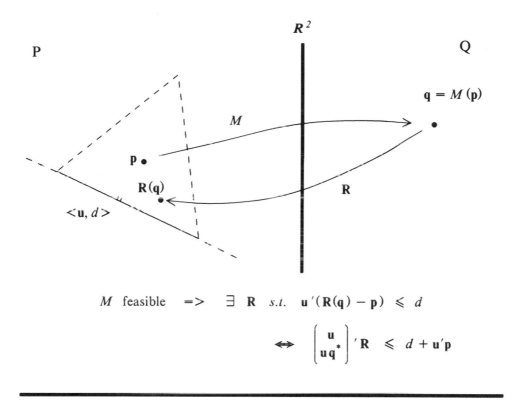

$$M \text{ feasible} \implies \exists \; \mathbf{R} \;\; s.t. \;\; \mathbf{u}'(\mathbf{R}(\mathbf{q}) - \mathbf{p}) \leqslant d$$

$$\Longleftrightarrow \begin{bmatrix} \mathbf{u} \\ \mathbf{u}\mathbf{q}^* \end{bmatrix}'\mathbf{R} \;\leqslant\; d + \mathbf{u}'\mathbf{p}$$

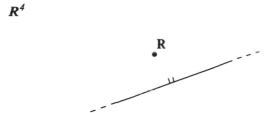

Figure 4-1. A linear noise constraint for a matched point determines a linear constraint in registration space (see Lemma 5-2 for derivation).

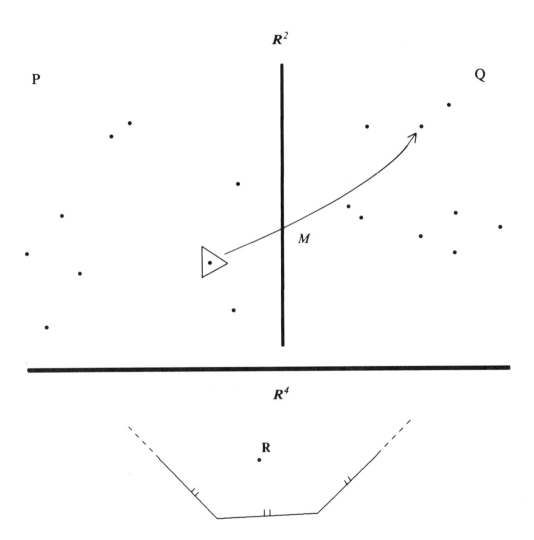

Figure 4 - 2.   Each point matched by *M* determines a set of registration con-
                 straints on **R**.

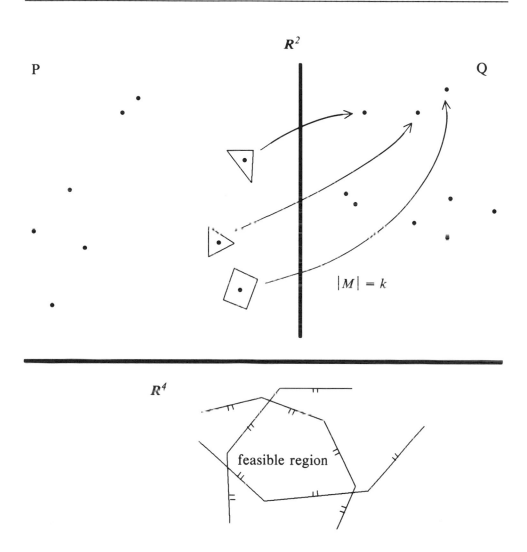

Figure 4-3.   Matching M is feasible if there is a non-empty feasible region in registration space.

order: $\mathbf{q}_1 \mathbf{q}_2 \cdots \mathbf{q}_n$.

We propose to explore a tree of partial matchings in depth-first order, so that, for any matching M, all shorter prefixes of M are examined earlier than M (see Figure 4-4). One possible such *exploration order* is lexicographic order [19]: *e.g.*, for $n=3$:

    1 12 123 13 132 2 21 213 23 231 3 31 312 32 321.

Each matching will specify a set of linear inequality constraints on **R**, which is tested in turn for feasibility. If a partial matching is found to be infeasible, then all matchings with this as a prefix must also be infeasible, and need not be examined -- they and their descendants in the tree are effectively pruned.

We will assume throughout the thesis that the search tree is to be *exhausted*: that is, the search continues until *all* successful matchings are found.

The time complexity of this algorithm can be broken into two contributions: the size of the tree, and the cost of testing feasibility. A reason for considering these separately is that the size of the tree is independent of the method used to test for feasibility, while the cost of testing depends both on the size of the tree and the testing method. The size of the tree is equal to the number of matchings tested, and is determined by the geometry of the model, instance, and noise polygons, and the comparison and exploration orders.

4.2. Number of Matchings Tested

Let $f(n,k)$ be the number of feasible matchings of size k for a given P, Q, noise constraints, and comparison and exploration order. (Define $f(n,0) = 1$.) Then the number of "successful" (feasible total) matchings is $f(n,n)$. Let $F(n) \equiv \sum_{k=1}^{n} f(n,k)$, the total number of feasible matchings. Every prefix of a feasible matching is of course feasible, so if $f(n,k) \geqslant 1$ then $f(n,j) \geqslant 1$ for all $j < k$.

Let $t(n,k)$ denote the number of matchings of size k tested for feasibility, and $T(n) \equiv \sum_{k=1}^{n} t(n,k)$, the total number of matchings tested.

4.2.1. Lower bounds

If a partial matching of size k is feasible, then $n - k$ successor matchings of size $k + 1$ are candidates to be tested next. If an exploration order is used in which *all* candidates are tested (such as lexicographic order), then

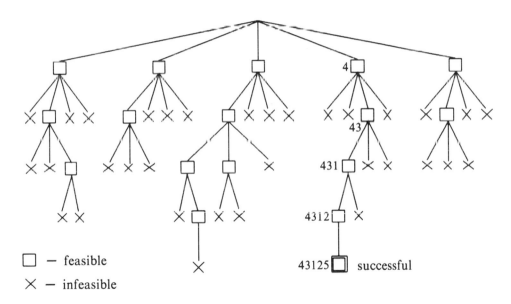

☐ — feasible

✕ — infeasible

Figure 4 - 4.   Depth-first search of a tree of partial matchings, pruned by feasibility tests.

$t(n,k) = (n-k+1) f(n,k-1)$. Thus, in the case that there are any successful matchings $(f(n,n) \geqslant 1)$, then a lower bound on the total number of matchings tested is:

$$T(n) \geqslant \sum_{k=1}^{n} (n-k+1) = \Omega(n^2) .$$

We have not found a way to test asymptotically fewer matchings, even in the expected case. However, in Chapter 9, we will describe a method for very efficiently testing all but a linear number of matchings overall.

4.2.2. Upper bounds

Any general discussion of upper bounds must consider a wide range of model point arrangements, noise constraints, and comparison and exploration orders. First, we consider some effects of noise.

4.2.2.1. High noise

In the extreme case where noise constraints are so loose that each model point falls within every noise polygon, $f(n,n) = n!$ and $T(n) = O(n^n)$ (assuming, as always, that we persist in the search until all successful matchings are found). This is symptomatic of a uselessly inaccurate feature extractor.

4.2.2.2. Zero noise

Another extreme case, where noise is absent, may at first glance also seem uninteresting, since some noise is unavoidable in practice. However, it is possible in this case to analyze the worst-case effect on $F(n)$ of symmetry and recurring subpatterns in highly regular patterns -- whereas, for the general non-zero noise case, this appears to be very difficult to analyze. We have found that, even for highly regular patterns, the total number of feasible matchings is only a low-order polynomial in n (Chapter 6).

Also, for many regular patterns, we have found general strategies which dramatically reduce the number of feasible matchings. It is easy in the zero-noise case to compare the improvement resulting from these strategies. It is our experience that these strategies also improve performance on more commonly-occurring, less regular patterns.

4.2.2.3. Moderate noise

The intermediate case of what we will call "moderate" noise is for practical purposes the most interesting. Informally, we consider noise moderate when it is non-zero but small compared to interpoint distances, so that noise polygons are likely to be disjoint. Here average-case analysis of behavior, rather than worst-case, is appropriate. In Chapter 7, we will propose a class of random patterns and noise, and, in Chapters 8 & 9, the expected behavior of the algorithm on the class is (partially) analyzed, and the notion of "moderate" noise made precise.

4.3. Cost of Feasibility Testing

We have implemented feasibility testing using both the Simplex algorithm and the Soviet ellipsoid algorithm. They both operate correctly (and of course identically) in their exploration of the tree of feasible matchings. However, their data structures and algorithms are different, and we find that the ellipsoid algorithm has some natural advantages over Simplex in this application.

4.3.1. Simplex algorithm

The Simplex algorithm [9], while known to require exponential time on specially-contrived instances [18], nevertheless enjoys a reputation for efficiency in practice [26]. In our application, the system of linear inequalities to be tested is put into standard form, artificial variables are introduced, and, using Revised Simplex, an attempt is made to drive them out of the basis. If this succeeds, the program returns the feasible basis from which the feasible registration can be computed. If it fails, then the system is infeasible.

For a matching of size k, there are $\Theta(k)$ constraints. In standard form, the Simplex tableau has $\Theta(k)$ rows and columns. Under these circumstances, a pivot requires $\Theta(k^2)$ arithmetic operations. Our experience using small triangular noise polygons suggests that the number of pivots required by Simplex grows at rate proportional to (in fact, roughly twice) the number of inequality constraints (see $n=9$ points-in-a-line results in Figure 4-5). This is similar to reported behavior of Simplex on other "real-world" problems [34]. Thus $\Theta(k^3)$ arithmetic operations are required to test feasibility of a partial matching of size k. In practice, it may be possible to conserve pivots while descending the tree, by adding new constraints (with slack variables for those not currently satisfied) to the current tableau.

Space requirements for the inverse-basis matrix used in testing a k-matching are $\Theta(k^2)$ real numbers, and each node along the search path will require its own full copy of the matrix. The total space required to descend the tree using Simplex is thus $\Theta(n^3)$.

4.3.2. Soviet ellipsoid algorithm

The Soviet ellipsoid algorithm [18], while provably polynomial-time in general, nevertheless has often been observed to run more slowly than Simplex on linear programming search problems. However, as suggested to us by Karl Lieberherr [25], the ellipsoid algorithm might be superior to Simplex when only a feasibility decision is required. We will show that this is true in the context of our problem. We have also found other features of the ellipsoid algorithm that recommend it for this application.

The ellipsoid algorithm works as follows: to test a set of linear inequality constraints on registrations in R^4, one must first provide an *initial ellipsoid* (say $\mathbf{E}_0$) which is guaranteed to enclose the entire feasible region, if any (see Figure 4-6). Take the existence of these initial ellipsoids on faith, for now; later, in Chapter 7, a method for constructing them as needed will be given.

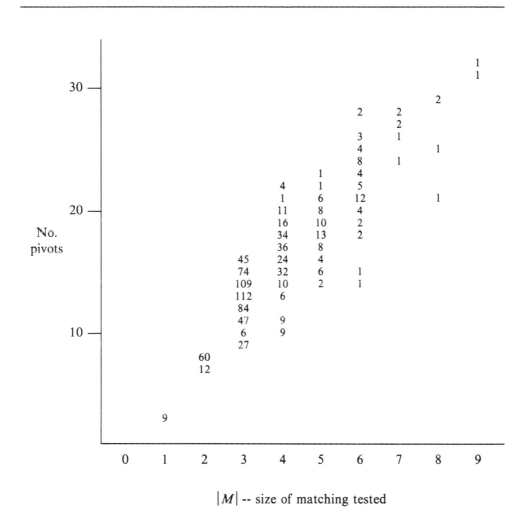

$|M|$ -- size of matching tested

Figure 4 - 5.   Number of Simplex pivots as a function of $|M|$ ($n = 9$, points-in-a-line pattern).

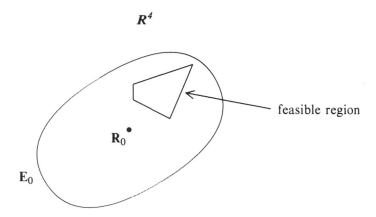

R^4

R_0

E_0

feasible region

Figure 4-6.   Initial state of feasibility testing by the Soviet ellipsoid method.

We will use the center R_0 of the ellipsoid as a probe point to be tested against the set of constraints determined by the matching. If R_0 satisfies them all, then the system has been proved feasible, and the algorithm reports success. Otherwise, test whether the entire volume of E_0 falls outside of every constraint — in this case, the feasible set is in fact empty, and the algorithm reports failure.

The last remaining case is that the volume of the ellipsoid is cut by some constraint which the center does *not* satisfy — it is then possible to *contract* E_0 in such a way that the resulting smaller ellipsoid E_1 encloses exactly the part of E_0 that does satisfy the constraint (see Figure 4-7). E_1, therefore, is guaranteed in its turn to enclose the entire feasible region, if any.

A crucial property of the geometry of d-dimensional ellipsoids is that each contraction   is   guaranteed   to   shrink   volume   by   at   least   the   factor

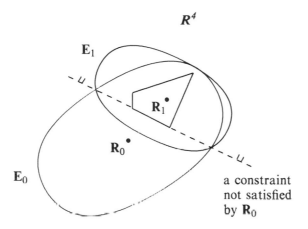

R⁴

R^4

Figure 4-7   One contraction of the ellipsoid.

$$\sigma \equiv e^{-\frac{1}{2(d+1)}} < 1 \ [18].$$ In our application, $d = 4$, so the ellipsoid volume shrinks by at least the factor $\sigma \approx 0.905$. This minimum shrinkage occurs only as the unsatisfied constraint comes arbitrarily close to R_0; the shrinkage is much greater for constraints a little distant from R_0.

Thus we can iterate this procedure: test the constraints against the current ellipsoid center; if not feasible, test constraints against the ellipsoid volume; if not infeasible, contract the ellipsoid. At each iteration, the volume of the ellipsoid decreases. Thus it is clear that the algorithm must eventually terminate, reporting either feasibility or infeasibility.

Now, we adapt this method to test feasibility of matchings, as follows. Recall that matchings are associated with nodes of a depth-first search tree. When we are about to test a $(k+1)$-matching M^{k+1}, we already know that its predecessor k-matching M^k is feasible. Thus the set of $O(k)$ "old" registration constraints, determined by M^k, has been shown to be feasible, and resulting from that demonstration is an ellipsoid $\mathbf{E}^k$ whose center, $\mathbf{R}^k$, is in fact a feasible registration under them.

The newly-matched, $(k+1)$th pair of points determines $O(1)$ "new" constraints which must now be tested (see Figure 4-8). First, $\mathbf{R}^k$ is checked against the new constraints only: if it satisfies them, then M^{k+1} has been proved feasible, in $O(1)$ time[3] — we say M^{k+1} is *immediately feasible*. If not, the new constraints are compared to the old ellipsoid $\mathbf{E}^k$'s volume: if any one of them excludes its entire volume, then M^{k+1} has been found infeasible, also in $O(1)$ time — we say M^{k+1} is *immediately infeasible*.

If neither case holds, then one of the unsatisfied constraints can be used to contract $\mathbf{E}^k$, and further testing continues as described earlier, but using *all* $O(k+1)$ constraints, both old and new. Eventually the current ellipsoid shrinks in volume until M^{k+1} is shown to be feasible or infeasible.

Each contraction requires computing the next ellipsoid in $O(1)$ time, then testing $O(k+1)$ constraints against the new ellipsoid, in $O(k+1)$ time. Thus the cost of testing feasibility is proportional to the total number of matchings tested plus the total cost of ellipsoid contractions. This fact will simplify our analysis of runtime complexity.

Preserving the state of computation at each node of the search tree (useful for backtracking) is space-efficient. The current ellipsoid is represented by a data structure of small constant size (20 real numbers). Thus the space required to descend the search tree using the Soviet ellipsoid algorithm is $O(n)$.

---

[3]   Measured in floating-point arithmetic operations: a random access machine (RAM) model of computation [33] is used throughout the thesis.

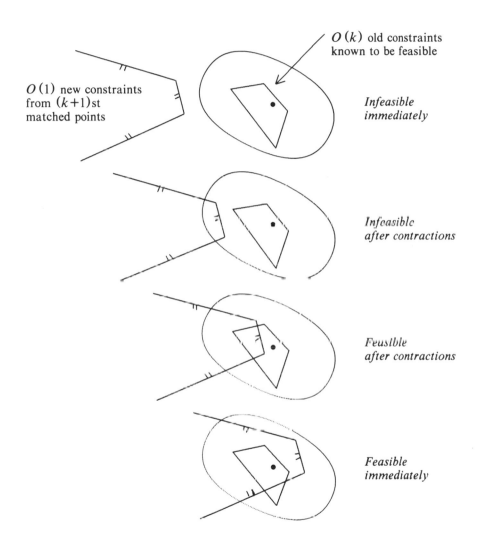

O(k) old constraints
known to be feasible

O(1) new constraints
from (k+1)st
matched points

Infeasible
immediately

Infeasible
after contractions

Feasible
after contractions

Feasible
immediately

Figure 4-8.   Cases during feasibility testing of a (k+1)-matching.

Later, we will point out other advantages of the ellipsoid representation, often due to its ability to concisely characterize intricate feasible regions. While the geometry of an ellipsoid can be explicitly described in $\Theta(1)$ space, the geometry of a feasible region requires $\Theta(n)$ space for only an *implicit* representation — and, to explicitly enumerate the vertices of the feasible polytope could require $\Theta(2^n)$ space in the worst case.

CHAPTER 5.

Geometry of Registrations & Ellipsoids

We will now set out some notational conventions and the elementary geometry of 2-D and 4-D linear inequality constraints, registrations, feasible regions, and ellipsoids.

5.1. Notation

We will use the following notational conventions:

i, j, k, etc.	integers
x, p_y, Δp, ϵ, etc.	scalar real variables
M, D, etc.	matchings or constant scalars
$\mathbf{p}$, $\mathbf{q}_j$, $\bar{\mathbf{p}}$, $\boldsymbol{\epsilon}$, etc.	vectors $\in \mathbf{R}^2$ (points)
$\mathbf{R}$, $\Delta \mathbf{R}$, $\tilde{\mathbf{R}}$, etc.	vectors $\in \mathbf{R}^4$ or matrices

5.2. Points

Conventional notation for 2-D vectors such as points include:

$$\mathbf{p} \equiv \begin{bmatrix} p_x \\ p_y \end{bmatrix} \qquad \| \mathbf{p} \| \equiv \sqrt{p_x^2 + p_y^2} \quad .$$

In addition to vector addition and subtraction, we will use complex multiplication[1], represented by concatenation:

$$\mathbf{p}\mathbf{q} \equiv \begin{bmatrix} p_x q_x - p_y q_y \\ p_y q_x + p_x q_y \end{bmatrix} \quad .$$

---

[1] "Complex" since it is equivalent to multiplication of the corresponding complex numbers where the x-component is taken to be the real part, and the y-component the imaginary part. We will make frequent tacit use of the fact that the set of 2-D vectors is a field under vector addition and complex multiplication.

Denote the complex conjugate of $\mathbf{p}$ by $\mathbf{p}^* \equiv \begin{bmatrix} p_x \\ -p_y \end{bmatrix}$. The multiplicative inverse

$\mathbf{p}^{-1}$ for a vector $\mathbf{p} \neq \begin{bmatrix} 0 \\ 0 \end{bmatrix}$ is given by $\mathbf{p}^* / \| \mathbf{p} \|^2$. Note that $\| \mathbf{p}\mathbf{q} \| = \| \mathbf{p} \| \| \mathbf{q} \|$.

Scalar product of two vectors will be written $\mathbf{p}'\mathbf{q} \equiv p_x q_x + p_y q_y$. It is easy to verify the useful fact that $\mathbf{p}'(\mathbf{q}\mathbf{r}) = (\mathbf{p}\mathbf{q}^*)'\mathbf{r}$.

5.3. Registrations

A registration $\mathbf{R}$ has two interpretations: as a vector $\in \mathbf{R}^4$, and as an affine transformation of the $\mathbf{R}^2$ plane. When $\mathbf{R}$ is interpreted as a vector, we use the notation

$$\mathbf{R} \equiv \begin{bmatrix} r_x \\ r_y \\ r_1 \\ r_2 \end{bmatrix} \quad .$$

In its role as an affine transformation of the $\mathbf{R}^2$ plane, we write

$$\mathbf{R}(\mathbf{p}) \equiv \begin{bmatrix} r_x \\ r_y \end{bmatrix} + \begin{bmatrix} r_1 & -r_2 \\ r_2 & r_1 \end{bmatrix} \mathbf{p}$$

It is often convenient to treat separately the translation (r_x, r_y) components from the scale and rotation components (r_1, r_2), so we have the special notation:

$$\mathbf{r}_{xy} \equiv \begin{bmatrix} r_x \\ r_y \end{bmatrix} \qquad \mathbf{r}_{12} \equiv \begin{bmatrix} r_1 \\ r_2 \end{bmatrix}$$

With these, we can compactly express the action of registration $\mathbf{R}$ using complex multiplication:

$$\mathbf{R}(\mathbf{p}) = \mathbf{r}_{xy} + \mathbf{r}_{12}\mathbf{p}$$

When r_1 and r_2 are not both 0, registration $\mathbf{R}$ has an inverse $\mathbf{R}^{-1}$, such that $\mathbf{R}^{-1}(\mathbf{R}(\mathbf{p})) = \mathbf{p}$ for every $\mathbf{p}$, given by

$$\mathbf{R}^{-1}(\mathbf{p}) \;=\; \frac{\mathbf{p} - \mathbf{r}_{xy}}{\mathbf{r}_{l2}} \quad . \tag{5-1}$$

For brevity's sake, we often use this non-standard notation for $\mathbf{R}$:

$$\mathbf{R} \;\equiv\; \begin{pmatrix} \mathbf{r}_{xy} \\ \mathbf{r}_{l2} \end{pmatrix} \quad .$$

We apply $\| \cdot \|$ and scalar product to registrations in the usual way, and we note they may be computed as follows:

$$\| \mathbf{R} \| \;=\; \sqrt{\| \mathbf{r}_{xy} \|^2 + \| \mathbf{r}_{l2} \|^2}$$

$$\mathbf{R}'\mathbf{S} \;=\; \mathbf{r}_{xy}'\mathbf{s}_{xy} + \mathbf{r}_{l2}'\mathbf{s}_{12}$$

We give a conventional name, r_s, to the scale factor $\| \mathbf{r}_{l2} \|$ resulting from $\mathbf{R}$. Since registrations are affine, these properties hold:

$$\text{If} \quad \mathbf{S} \;=\; \sum_{i=1}^{k} \mathbf{R}_i \quad \text{then} \quad \mathbf{S}(\mathbf{p}) \;=\; \sum_{i=1}^{k} \mathbf{R}_i(\mathbf{p})$$

$$\mathbf{R}\Big(\frac{1}{k} \sum_{i=1}^{k} \mathbf{p}_i \Big) \;=\; \frac{1}{k} \sum_{i=1}^{k} \mathbf{R}(\mathbf{p}_i) \tag{5-2}$$

5.3.1. Power of registrations

Registrations are powerful enough to superimpose perfectly any pair of distinct instance points onto any pair of model points, as shown in this Lemma.

Lemma 5-1. The unique registration $\mathbf{R}$ superimposing any two distinct instance points $\mathbf{q}_a$ and $\mathbf{q}_b$ onto any two model points $\mathbf{p}_a$ and $\mathbf{p}_b$ with zero pointwise error is given by

$$\mathbf{R} \;=\; \begin{pmatrix} \overline{\mathbf{p}} - \dfrac{\Delta \mathbf{p}}{\Delta \mathbf{q}}\, \overline{\mathbf{q}} \\[2ex] \dfrac{\Delta \mathbf{p}}{\Delta \mathbf{q}} \end{pmatrix}$$

where $\overline{\mathbf{p}} \equiv \tfrac{1}{2}(\mathbf{p}_a + \mathbf{p}_b)$, $\Delta \mathbf{p} \equiv \mathbf{p}_b - \mathbf{p}_a$, and $\overline{\mathbf{q}}$ and $\Delta \mathbf{q}$ are defined analogously using $\mathbf{q}_a$ and $\mathbf{q}_b$.

Proof. $\mathbf{R}$ can be shown to work by substitution: for example,

$$\mathbf{R}(\mathbf{q}_a) \;=\; \mathbf{r}_{xy} + \mathbf{r}_{12}\mathbf{q}_a \;=\; (\bar{\mathbf{p}} - \frac{\Delta\mathbf{p}}{\Delta\mathbf{q}}\bar{\mathbf{q}}) + (\frac{\Delta\mathbf{p}}{\Delta\mathbf{q}})\,\mathbf{q}_a$$

$$=\; \bar{\mathbf{p}} + \frac{\Delta\mathbf{p}}{\Delta\mathbf{q}}(\mathbf{q}_a - \bar{\mathbf{q}}) \;=\; \bar{\mathbf{p}} + \frac{\Delta\mathbf{p}}{\Delta\mathbf{q}}(\frac{-\Delta\mathbf{q}}{2}) \;=\; \bar{\mathbf{p}} - \frac{\Delta\mathbf{p}}{2} \;=\; \mathbf{p}_a$$

$\mathbf{R}$ is unique since it is a solution of a non-singular system of linear equalities with four degrees of freedom (the coordinates of $\mathbf{p}_1$ and $\mathbf{p}_2$) for an equal number of unknowns (the parameters of $\mathbf{R}$). ∎

Note that the instance points $\mathbf{q}_a$ and $\mathbf{q}_b$ need to be distinct if the model points $\mathbf{p}_a$ and $\mathbf{p}_b$ are distinct: otherwise, no zero-error registration exists. If both $\mathbf{p}_a = \mathbf{p}_b$ and $\mathbf{q}_a = \mathbf{q}_b$, then the zero-error registration is simply a translation.

5.3.2. Registration constraints

As mentioned in Chapter 4, a matching M implies a set of linear inequality constraints on registrations. Now we derive this explicitly. Suppose $M(\mathbf{p}) = \mathbf{q}$, and let $< \mathbf{u}, d >$ be a noise constraint for $\mathbf{p}$. Then for M to be feasible, there must exist a registration $\mathbf{R}$ such that:

$$\mathbf{u}'(\mathbf{R} - \mathbf{p}) \;\leqslant\; d$$

or,

$$\mathbf{u}'\mathbf{R} \;\leqslant\; d + \mathbf{u}'\mathbf{p} \tag{5-3}$$

Now,

$$\mathbf{u}'\mathbf{R} \;=\; \mathbf{u}'\mathbf{r}_{xy} + \mathbf{u}'(\mathbf{r}_{12}\mathbf{q}) \;=\; \mathbf{u}'\mathbf{r}_{xy} + (\mathbf{u}\mathbf{q}^*)'\mathbf{r}_{12}$$

so that we have:

Lemma 5-2. For any P, Q, matching M (not necessarily feasible), matched pair $\mathbf{q} = M(\mathbf{p})$, and noise constraint for $\mathbf{p}$ specified by $< \mathbf{u}, d >$, the corresponding constraint on a feasible registration $\mathbf{R}$ is given by

$$\begin{bmatrix} \mathbf{u} \\ \mathbf{u}\,\mathbf{q}^* \end{bmatrix}\,'\,\mathbf{R} \quad \leqslant \quad d \; + \; \mathbf{u}\,'\,\mathbf{p} \quad \blacksquare \tag{5-4}$$

It is often interesting to determine how closely a constraint hyperplane can approach a given registration $\tilde{\mathbf{R}}$ ($\in R^4$), so let us replace $\mathbf{R}$ by $\tilde{\mathbf{R}} + \delta\mathbf{R}$ in equation (5-3):

$$\mathbf{u}\,'(\,(\tilde{\mathbf{R}}+\delta\mathbf{R})\,)(\mathbf{q}) \quad \leqslant \quad d + \mathbf{u}\,'\mathbf{p}$$

$$\mathbf{u}\,'(\,\tilde{\mathbf{R}}(\mathbf{q})+\delta\mathbf{R}(\mathbf{q})\,) \quad \leqslant \quad d + \mathbf{u}\,'\mathbf{p}$$

$$\mathbf{u}\,'\delta\mathbf{R}(\mathbf{q}) \quad \leqslant \quad d + \mathbf{u}\,'\mathbf{p} - \mathbf{u}\,'\tilde{\mathbf{R}}(\mathbf{q})$$

Thus the linear inequality constraint on $\delta\mathbf{R}$ is:

$$\begin{bmatrix} \mathbf{u} \\ \mathbf{u}\,\mathbf{q}^* \end{bmatrix}\,'\,\delta\mathbf{R} \quad \leqslant \quad d + \mathbf{u}\,'(\,\mathbf{p} - \tilde{\mathbf{R}}(\mathbf{q})\,) \tag{5-5}$$

Now, since $\mathbf{u}$ is a unit vector,

$$\left\| \begin{bmatrix} \mathbf{u} \\ \mathbf{u}\,\mathbf{q}^* \end{bmatrix} \right\| \quad = \quad \sqrt{1 + \|\mathbf{q}\|^2}$$

Dividing both sides of (5-5) by this magnitude, we have, on the left side, a unit vector acting on $\delta\mathbf{R}$, and thus, on the right, we have the closest approach of the hyperplane to $\delta\mathbf{R}$, proving:

Lemma 5-3. For any P, Q, matching M (not necessarily feasible), matched pair $\mathbf{q} = M(\mathbf{p})$, and noise constraint for $\mathbf{p}$ specified by $< \mathbf{u}, d >$, where $\mathbf{u}$ is a unit vector, then, the (signed) closest approach of the corresponding registration constraint hyperplane to an arbitrary registration $\tilde{\mathbf{R}}$ is given by

$$\frac{d + \mathbf{u}\,'(\mathbf{p} - \tilde{\mathbf{R}}(\mathbf{q}))}{\sqrt{1 + \|\mathbf{q}\|^2}} \tag{5-6}$$

and non-negative values indicate that $\tilde{\mathbf{R}}$ satisfies the constraint. $\blacksquare$

5.4. Ellipsoids

We will use ellipsoids in R^4 to enclose sets of registrations. Formally, an ellipsoid $\mathbf{E}$ is an ordered pair $< \tilde{\mathbf{R}}, \mathbf{A} >$ where $\tilde{\mathbf{R}}$ is the center of the ellipsoid and $\mathbf{A}$ is a symmetric positive-definite 4×4 matrix. A registration $\mathbf{R}$ lies within the 4-D volume of the ellipsoid iff $\mathbf{R}$ satisfies the quadratic inequality

$$(\mathbf{R} - \tilde{\mathbf{R}})^T \, \mathbf{A}^{-1} \, (\mathbf{R} - \tilde{\mathbf{R}}) \;\leqslant\; 1 \quad .$$

The 4-D volume $Vol\,(\; < \tilde{\mathbf{R}}, \mathbf{A} > \;)$ of ellipsoid $< \tilde{\mathbf{R}}, \mathbf{A} >$ is given by $\dfrac{\pi^2}{6}\sqrt{\det(\mathbf{A})}$.

Suppose we are given an upper bound on the magnitude of $\delta\mathbf{R} = \mathbf{R} - \tilde{\mathbf{R}}$, in the form $\| \delta\mathbf{R} \| \leqslant B$; then an ellipsoid enforcing that bound on $\mathbf{R}$ is $< \tilde{\mathbf{R}}, B^2\mathbf{I} >$, where $\mathbf{I}$ is the identity matrix. This is simply a 4-D sphere of radius B, and its volume is $\dfrac{\pi^2}{6}B^4$.

Suppose we are given upper bounds on the magnitude of the two vector components of $\delta\mathbf{R} = \mathbf{R} - \tilde{\mathbf{R}}$, that is, $\| \delta\mathbf{r}_{xy} \| \leqslant B_{xy}$, and $\| \delta\mathbf{r}_{12} \| \leqslant B_{12}$, then an ellipsoid enforcing the bounds on $\mathbf{R}$ is $< \tilde{\mathbf{R}}, \mathbf{B} >$, where

$$\mathbf{B} \;=\; \begin{pmatrix} 2\,B_{xy}^2 & 0 & 0 & 0 \\ 0 & 2\,B_{xy}^2 & 0 & 0 \\ 0 & 0 & 2\,B_{12}^2 & 0 \\ 0 & 0 & 0 & 2\,B_{12}^2 \end{pmatrix}$$

and the volume of the ellipsoid is $\dfrac{2\,\pi^2}{3}B_{xy}^2\,B_{12}^2$.

CHAPTER 6

Worst-Case Number
of Feasible Matchings

We have been able to analyze worst-case asymptotic number of feasible matchings for certain regular patterns in the limiting case of zero noise.[1] We can show that for a large class of highly regular patterns, this number is a low-order polynomial in the number of pattern points. Also, the analysis suggests methods for bounding registrations that will prove to be useful later in the analysis of expected-case behavior.

6.1. Zero-noise Conditions

Let us say that two point patterns are *similar* if they can be registered perfectly, *i.e.* with zero noise. If for a given model pattern, point-wise noise is constrained to zero, then the number of feasible k-matchings $f(n,k)$ equals the number of subsets of P of size k that are similar to the first k points of P, in the given comparison order.

For any pattern, $f(n, 1) = n$ and $f(n, 2) = n^2$. We will analyze the behavior of $F(n) = \sum_{k=1}^{n} f(n,k)$ for certain regular patterns.

Consider a pattern of points arranged uniformly on the circumference of a circle, with comparison order simply order around the circumference. Then, $f(n,k) = n$ and so $F(n) = O(n^2)$.

---

[1] We do not suggest using our algorithm in this case, since it can be solved in the worst-case in *O(n log n)* time by polar-encoding both P and Q (assumed rational), sorting into circular lists on <angle,radius^2>, converting to the form <Δ-angle,radius^2>, and finally comparing the lists for perfect match using one of the *O(n)* string-matching algorithms [33]. Perfect match is possible in principle since, with a little ingenuity, the encodings can be done in rational arithmetic.

Consider a pattern of points arranged in a straight line, uniformly spaced, with comparison order simply order along the line; then

$$f(n,k) = 2 \sum_{s=1}^{\left\lfloor \frac{n-1}{k-1} \right\rfloor} (n - s(k-1))$$

where s is a registration scale factor. This is $O(n^2/k)$ asymptotically, and the total number of feasible matchings is

$$F(n) = O(n^2 \log n) \quad . \tag{6-1}$$

Now consider highly regular array patterns, made up of many copies of a simple pattern, such as a triangle or square, growing to fill the plane. It may seem that, for these, $F(n)$ would grow faster than for other patterns, such as points-in-a-line, that seem simpler — but we will exhibit a large class of such patterns for which this is not the case.

Consider any sequence of patterns $< P_i >_{i=1,2,...}$, where $P_n = < \mathbf{p}_1, \mathbf{p}_2, ..., \mathbf{p}_n >$. Note that if $k < l$, then $P_k \subset P_l$. We will carry out our analysis in arbitrary d-dimensional Euclidean space[2], in such a way that $d=1$ describes the points-in-a-line case above, $d=2$ regular patterns in the plane, etc. We will require only that the patterns:

(i) *do not collapse*: for all P_n, the minimum interpoint distance equals $\| \mathbf{p}_1 - \mathbf{p}_2 \|$ and is scaled to equal 1 —

$$\| \mathbf{p}_1 - \mathbf{p}_2 \| = \min_{\substack{i,j=1,2,...,n \\ i \neq j}} \{ \| \mathbf{p}_i - \mathbf{p}_j \| \} = 1 \quad ;$$

(ii) *grow outward spherically*: all points of P_n are contained in a sphere about the "center" $\mathbf{p}_1$, of radius r_n such that $n = \Theta(r_n^d)$ — that is, there exist

---

[2] The results will be interesting principally for $d=1$ and $d=2$, since we will not increase the power of registrations with increasing d.

fixed "density" bounds D_0 and D_l so that $D_0 r_n^d \leqslant n \leqslant D_l r_n^d$, for all n — if a point lies inside this sphere, we say it lies "within the bounds of" P_n; and

(iii) *spread uniformly*: within the bounds of each P_n, every sphere of radius r, centered at a point of P_n, contains at most $D_l r^d$ points.

Properties (i) and (iii) hold for any pattern built up by simple replication of (or, tiling by) a fixed subpattern. Property (ii) permits the frequent occurrence of many subpatterns with high rotational symmetry. The convention that the absolute minimum interpoint distance is $\| \mathbf{p}_1 - \mathbf{p}_2 \| = 1$ simplifies analysis by bounding the scale of feasible registrations from above by unity.

By Lemma 5-1, we know that for any 2-matching there is a unique registration of zero error: that is, a 2-matching determines a similarity transformation. Thus we focus on matching only two points of P_k (its "center" $\mathbf{p}_1$, and the center's closest neighbor $\mathbf{p}_2$) to some two points in P_n (call them $\mathbf{p}_a$ and $\mathbf{p}_b$). Then $f(n,k)$ will equal the number of pairs $\mathbf{p}_a$, $\mathbf{p}_b$ in P_n that determine a feasible matching; that is, whose matching to $\mathbf{p}_1$ and $\mathbf{p}_2$ of P_k determines a registration that superimposes each point of P_k on some point in P_n.

Certainly, no matching is possible for a registration that locates any point of P_k outside the bounds of P_n. We can use this fact to bound r, the distance of $\mathbf{p}_a$ from the center of P_n, and, for each $\mathbf{p}_a$, bound the distance $s = \| \mathbf{p}_a - \mathbf{p}_b \|$. (Since $\| \mathbf{p}_1 - \mathbf{p}_2 \|$ is conventionally 1, s^{-1} gives the scale of the registration.)

Now r can range from 0 to $r_n - r_k$ — otherwise P_k, which cannot shrink (due to property (i)), will extend outside the bounds of P_n. For any r, s can range from 1, the minimum interpoint distance, to $(r_n - r)/r_k$ — otherwise the scaled P_k will grow so large that some point will extend beyond P_n. Let us call *2-possible* any matching whose $\mathbf{p}_a$ and $\mathbf{p}_b$ meet these minimal conditions for feasibility.

We can compute an upper bound on the number of 2-possible matchings. The number of points $\mathbf{p}_a$ between r and $r + dr$ is at most $(D_l d r^{d-1}) dr$ (from property (ii)). The total number of points $\mathbf{p}_b$ possible for any r is at most the number contained within a sphere of radius $(r_n - r)/r_k$, as we have seen. Thus the number of 2-possible matchings is bounded from above by the continuous function:

$$B(n,k) \quad = \quad \int_0^{r_n - r_k} \left[D_1 \, d \, r^{d-1} \right] \left[D_1 \left[\frac{r_n - r}{r_k} \right]^d \right] \, dr \qquad (6\text{-}2)$$

Substituting $t = r/r_n$ and $t_k = r_k/r_n$ yields

$$B(n,k) \quad = \quad \frac{D_1^2 \, d \, r_n^{2d}}{r_k^d} \int_0^{1 - t_k} t^{d-1} (1-t)^d \, dt$$

Now, $t \in [0, 1]$, so the value of the integral is no more than 1; thus

$$B(n,k) \quad \leqslant \quad \frac{D_1^2 \, d \, r_n^{2d}}{r_k^d}$$

Since any feasible matching must be 2-possible, this result bounds $f(n,k)$ from above. To investigate the asymptotic behavior of $F(n) = \sum_{k=1}^{n} f(n,k)$, we will bound the sum from above using

$$F(n) \quad \leqslant \quad f(n, 1) + f(n, 2) + \int_2^n B(n,k) \, dk \qquad . \qquad (6\text{-}3)$$

This holds since, for fixed n and $k \geqslant 2$, $B(n,k)$ is monotonic nonincreasing in k. We know that $f(n, 1) = n$ and $f(n, 2) = n^2$. From property (ii) we can derive $dk \leqslant D_1 \, d \, r_k^{d-1} \, dr_k$, so

$$\int_2^n B(n,k) \, dk \quad \leqslant \quad \int_{r_2}^{r_n} B(n,k) \, (D_1 \, d \, r_k^{d-1} \, dr_k)$$

$$= \quad D_1^3 \, d^2 \, r_n^{2d} \int_1^{r_n} \frac{1}{r_k} \, dr_k \quad = \quad D_1^3 \, d^2 \, r_n^{2d} \ln(r_n)$$

Now, from (ii), using the fact that $r_n \leqslant (n/D_0)^{1/d}$, we have, for any fixed dimension d,

$$F(n) \;\leqslant\; n + n^2 + D_l^3\, d^2 \left[\frac{n}{D_0}\right]^2 \left[\frac{1}{d}\, \ln\left[\frac{n}{D_0}\right]\right] \;=\; O(n^2\, \log n)$$

The $d=1$ case is, of course, the points-in-a-line case we worked through exactly, and the results agree: so this approximate derivation did not loosen the bound asymptotically. We know that $f(n, 2) = \Omega(n^2)$, so the upper bound for $d \geqslant 2$ seems to be fairly tight.

That the bound is fairly tight may seem surprising — after all, it was computed by constraining the geometry of only *two* pairs of points. It is plausible that, when the arrangement of *all* pairs are considered, there would be many more 2-possible matchings than feasible matchings.

However, we have found patterns for which every 2-possible k-matching is feasible. For example, the pattern made up of many repetitions of equilateral triangles has this property (for the proof, see the Appendix). Thus the $O(n^2 \log n)$ bound is tight.

We conjecture that no planar pattern can produce $F(n)$ growth worse than $O(n^2 \log n)$. If this is true, then the mere *arrangement* of model points cannot, in itself, cause the total number of feasible matchings to grow exponentially. Since many patterns encountered in practice will be less regular than the special cases we have constructed, we expect that the size of the search tree will typically be a low-order polynomial.

6.2. Prior Registration Constraints

If no constraints can be placed on registrations prior to matching feature points, then by Lemma 5-1 every matching of size 2 is feasible, and so $f(n, 2) = n(n-1) = \Theta(n^2)$.

However, this can often be reduced in practice by exploiting prior registration constraints. Any convex constraint can be approximated as closely as desired by a set of linear inequality constraints. These can be prefixed to each set of constraints implied by partial matchings, and the combined system tested for feasibility.

Some combined constraints can be concisely expressed in an *initial ellipsoid*, thus reducing the number of constraints that must be examined at each contraction.

6.2.1. Constraining translation

A straightforward and general method of constraining translation is to "match" the centroids of P and Q:

$$\bar{\mathbf{p}} \equiv \frac{1}{n} \sum_{i=1}^{n} \mathbf{p}_i \qquad \bar{\mathbf{q}} \equiv \frac{1}{n} \sum_{i=1}^{n} \mathbf{q}_i \ .$$

Recall from (2-1) that

$$\mathbf{R}(M(\mathbf{p}_i)) \ = \ \mathbf{p}_i + \boldsymbol{\epsilon}_i$$

where $\boldsymbol{\epsilon}_i$ is constrained by the system

$$\mathbf{U}_i \, \boldsymbol{\epsilon}_i \ \leqslant \ \mathbf{d}_i \ . \tag{6-4}$$

Trivially, $\sum_{i=1}^{n} \mathbf{R}(M(\mathbf{p}_i)) \ = \ \sum_{i=1}^{n} \mathbf{R}(\mathbf{q}_i)$, and, since $\mathbf{R}$ is affine,

$$\frac{1}{n} \sum_{i=1}^{n} \mathbf{R}(\mathbf{q}_i) \ = \ \mathbf{R}\left(\frac{1}{n} \sum_{i=1}^{n} \mathbf{q}_i \right) \ ;$$

thus we have

$$\mathbf{R}(\bar{\mathbf{q}}) \ = \ \bar{\mathbf{p}} + \frac{1}{n} \sum_{i=1}^{n} \boldsymbol{\epsilon}_i \ . \tag{6-5}$$

Call $\bar{\boldsymbol{\epsilon}} \equiv \frac{1}{n} \sum_{i=1}^{n} \boldsymbol{\epsilon}_i$ the *noise vector of the centroid* (see Figure 6-1).

The range of a scaled sum of vectors is the convolution of their scaled ranges [22]. The result of performing the convolution corresponding to (6-5) for all i is that $\bar{\boldsymbol{\epsilon}}$ must lie within a convex polygon in the plane of at most $\sum_{i=1}^{n} l_i = O(n)$

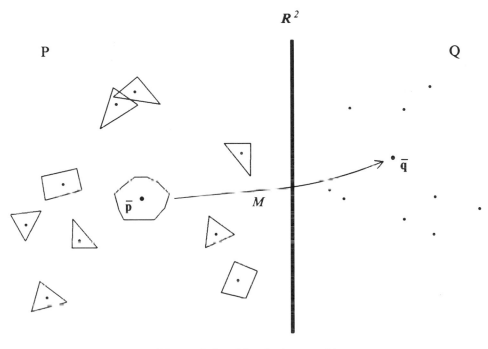

Figure 6-1.   Matched centroids.

sides. (This polygon can be precomputed for P in $O(n \ log \ n)$ time, by merging polygons' vertices in clockwise order.)

Note that the largest "radius" of the centroid noise polygon is no greater than the mean of the largest radii of the feature points' noise polygons, so the centroid's noise vectors all obey the same upper bound ϵ on magnitude as the feature points' noise vectors:

$$\| \bar{\epsilon} \| = \| \frac{1}{n} \sum_{i=1}^{n} \epsilon_i \| = \frac{1}{n} \| \sum_{i=1}^{n} \epsilon_i \| \leqslant \frac{1}{n} \sum_{i=1}^{n} \| \epsilon_i \| \leqslant \frac{n \epsilon}{n} = \epsilon \qquad \text{(6-6)}$$

If the centroids are "matched", prior to matching feature points, the extra $O(n)$ registration constraints implied will not alter which total matchings are found to be feasible, since they are redundant; but some matchings of size 2 will be found infeasible. The effect is to bound translation without bounding rotation or scale.[3]

For points-in-a-line under zero noise, this strategy has a dramatic effect: *all* matchings of size 2 are found infeasible except precisely those which are prefixes of feasible total matchings: thus the number of feasible matchings drops from $O(n^2 \log n)$ to $O(n)$.

6.2.2. Constraining scale

In many applications, scale is constant or, if variable, can be bounded from above. There will, for example, ordinarily be some fixed maximum distance of objects from the observing camera. If no *a priori* bound is known, one can be estimated from P and Q, as follows. Given P and its noise polygons, precompute, for each $\mathbf{p}_i$, the longest distance from the vertices of $\mathbf{p}_i$'s noise polygon to the vertices of $\bar{\mathbf{p}}$'s noise polygon, and call it r_i (see Figure 6-2). This is an upper bound on the "radial" distance $\| \mathbf{R}(M(\mathbf{p}_i)) - \mathbf{R}(\bar{\mathbf{q}}) \|$ for any feasible M and $\mathbf{R}$. Now,

$$\| \mathbf{R}(M(\mathbf{p}_i)) - \mathbf{R}(\bar{\mathbf{q}}) \| = r_s \cdot \| M(\mathbf{p}_i) - \bar{\mathbf{q}} \|$$

Then $\sum_{i=1}^{n} r_s \cdot \| M(\mathbf{p}_i) - \bar{\mathbf{q}} \| = r_s \cdot \sum_{j=1}^{n} \| \mathbf{q}_j - \bar{\mathbf{q}} \| \leqslant \sum_{i=1}^{n} r_i$, and thus an upper bound on scale for any feasible M and $\mathbf{R}$ is given by:

---

[3] Consider that without loss of generality we can translate both P and Q so that their centroids are at the origin *(0,0)*; then, under any R, any displacement of $\bar{\mathbf{q}}$ with respect to $\bar{\mathbf{p}}$ is due entirely to the translation parameters r_x, r_y. This idea is developed at length later, in Section 7.5.

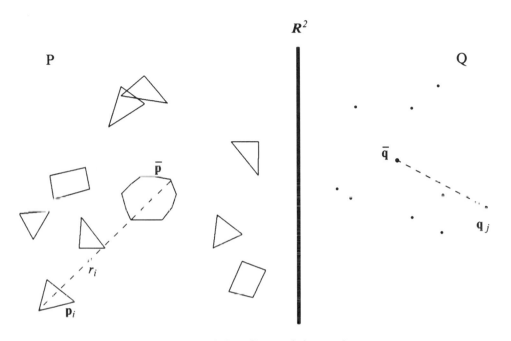

Figure 6-2.   Constraining scale.

$$\frac{\sum\limits_{i=1}^{n} r_i}{\sum\limits_{j=1}^{n} \| \mathbf{q}_j - \overline{\mathbf{q}} \|} \; .$$

The convex registration constraint

$$r_1^2 + r_2^2 \; \leqslant \; S_{max}^2 \;\; ,$$

enforces an upper bound S_{max} on scale. Given a model P and its (non-overlapping) noise polygons, it is easy to find two polygons which are "farthest apart" — that is, some pair of their vertices form a diameter of the set of all vertices of the polygons. Now, when choosing a comparison order on P, simply make $\mathbf{p}_1$ and $\mathbf{p}_2$ the feature points of these two polygons. Then, any matching of size 2, say $m_1 \, m_2$, is infeasible if

$$\frac{\| \mathbf{p}_1 - \mathbf{p}_2 \|}{\| \mathbf{q}_{m_1} - \mathbf{q}_{m_2} \|} \; > \; S_{max} \; .$$

In the limit case of an instance *at* scale S_{max}, under zero noise, no matching is feasible unless $\mathbf{q}_{m_1}$ and $\mathbf{q}_{m_2}$ form a diameter of Q. Among n points in the plane, only n pairs can form diameters [37]; thus the number of feasible matchings of size 2 drops from $O(n^2)$ in general to $O(n)$.

6.2.3. Constraining rotation

Given P and Q, it seems difficult in general to derive intrinsic constraints on rotation. (Perhaps second- or higher-order moments can be used to bound rotation here and in the case of more general affine transformations.) However, the feature extractor may provide, for some or all feature points, an estimate of orientation angle and worst-case bounds on the error of this estimate. In this case, a matching of two such points implies a range of feasible difference angles between P and Q which can be expressed as two linear inequality constraints perpendicular to the r_1-r_2 plane.

6.2.4. Combined constraints

The power of combining prior translation and scale constraints is dramatically evident in the points-in-a-line case under zero noise: no matchings, of any size, are found feasible except precisely those which are prefixes of the two feasible total matchings — the best possible result.

The limitations of this strategy are illustrated in the points-in-a-circle case: in spite of constraining translation and scale, $O(n^2)$ matchings are still feasible.

We conjecture that when combined constraints are used, then for *every* planar pattern, $F(n) = O(n^2)$.

CHAPTER 7.

Random Patterns

To investigate the behavior of our algorithm on "average" patterns, we will propose a class of random patterns, and then analyze the algorithm in the expected-case. The principal constraint on the class will be an intuitive notion of "moderate" noise: the size of worst-case pointwise noise will be bounded from above so that confusion between feature points is unlikely — although we permit this to occur. A technical concern is that the scale of noise must be related to n, the size of patterns, so that the effects of noise are comparable among patterns of different size.

Some classical results of geometric probability applied to this class are presented, and the geometry of feasible regions is described. The prior constraint strategies introduced in section 6.2 are analyzed for this class. These results will be used in the following two chapters, which prove upper bounds on aspects of expected behavior of the algorithm.

7.1. A Class of Random Patterns

A *random model* P of size n is chosen as follows. Choose a radius $\rho > 0$, thus fixing the geometrical scale of the pattern. Also choose an upper bound on pointwise noise $\epsilon > 0$. (The relation between these will be discussed in the next section.)

Choose a set of n points $< \mathbf{p}_i >_{i=1,\dots,n}$ independently and uniformly in the interior of a circle of radius ρ centered at the origin (see Figure 7-1). For each point $\mathbf{p}_i$, construct a regular polygon of $l_{\max}$ sides, with the vertices at a distance ϵ from the origin, rotated at an angle chosen uniformly in $[0, 2\pi]$ (see Figure 7-2). (Recall from section 1.5 that $l_{\max}$ is the maximum number of sides permitted in noise polygons, and is a fixed small integer.) The sides of the regular $l_{\max}$-gon

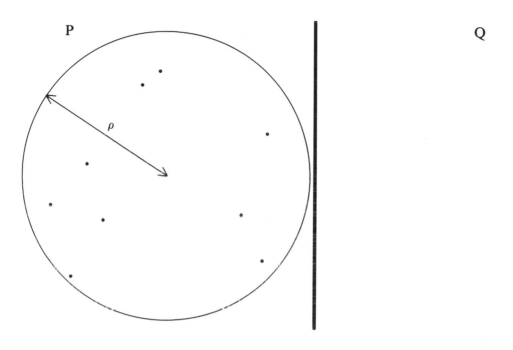

Figure 7 - 1.   Choose model points independently and uniformly within a circle
of radius ρ about the origin.

determine the linear inequality constraints $< U_i, d_i >$ on pointwise noise for this
point.

A *random instance* Q of a random model P is chosen as follows. First, for
each point p_i in P, choose a random noise vector $\hat{\epsilon}_i$ uniformly within the area of
p_i's noise polygon (see Figure 7-3). The ordered set $< p_i + \hat{\epsilon}_i >_{i=1,...,n}$ is called
the *noisy model*.

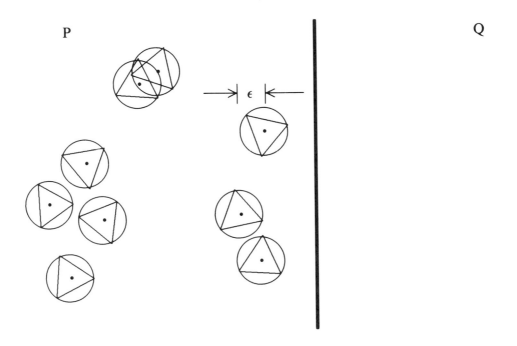

Figure 7 - 2.   Construct noise polygons centered at the model points, of l_{max}
                    sides (here, 3), and radius ϵ, at random orientations.

Throughout our analysis, we will assume that a *fixed* registration $\hat{\mathbf{R}}$ is used in generating an instance from the model, subject only to the restriction that it is invertible (r_1 and r_2 are not both zero). We use this inverse to misregister the noisy model, forming the ordered set $< \hat{\mathbf{R}}^{-1}(\mathbf{p}_i + \hat{\boldsymbol{\epsilon}}_i) >_{i=1,...,n}$ (also see Figure 7-3).

Finally, choose a random n-permutation $\hat{M}$ (uniformly over all n-permutations) and use it to shuffle the order of these points as follows:

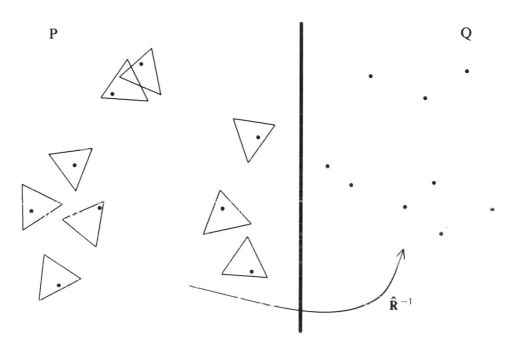

Figure 7 - 3.   Choose noisy model points uniformly within polygons, and mis-
                    register, forming the instance points.

$$\mathbf{q}_{\hat{M}(i)} \equiv \hat{\mathbf{R}}^{-1}(\mathbf{p}_i + \hat{\boldsymbol{\epsilon}}_i) \quad .$$

For convenience, we view $\hat{M}$ both as a permutation of the indices $< 1, 2,..., n >$ (writing $\hat{M}(i) = j$) and as a matching of point sets (writing $\hat{M}(\mathbf{p}_i) = \mathbf{q}_j$). This yields a random instance $Q = <\mathbf{q}_j>_{j=1,...,n}$.

There is, admittedly, no consensus among workers in the field of pattern recognition on a "representative" class of point patterns. Thus we have felt free to choose uniform distributions throughout, to simplify our analysis. That model points are uniformly distributed within a circle seems to us to represent a minimal and intuitive proposal. The assumption of uniform distribution of noisy images within the noise polygons may seen somewhat artificial, since it is natural to expect a centralizing tendency in practice. However, this assumption gives relatively pessimistic bounds, as described later in Chapter 8.

7.2. Asymptotic Effects of Noise

An important technical matter remaining is the asymptotic relation between the worst-case noise ϵ and the scale ρ of the model pattern, as n grows. If ϵ were to increase with respect to ρ, the expected number of pairs of noise polygons which overlap will increase, increasing the likelihood that the points involved will be confused during matching. We wish to limit the growth of such "confusion" as n increases, so that the effects of noise are comparable for different values of n.

How shall we make this precise? Let us say that a pair of model points are *confusable* with each other when their noise polygons overlap. We propose that, for asymptotic analysis of noise effects to be meaningful, the expected number of points confusable with one random model point must be bounded from above by a fixed number, for all n.

Lemma 7-1. If $\rho \geqslant 2\epsilon\sqrt{n/\kappa}$, then the expected number of model points confusable with a random model point is no more than κ.

Proof. For a pair of points $\mathbf{p}_i$ and $\mathbf{p}_j$ chosen at random from P, the probability that their noise polygons overlap is bounded above by the probability that $\mathbf{p}_i$ is closer to $\mathbf{p}_j$ than twice ϵ. This equals the probability that $\mathbf{p}_j$ lies within a circle of radius 2ϵ centered at $\mathbf{p}_i$. This, in turn, is bounded above by the ratio of areas of this circle to the circle from which $\mathbf{p}_j$ was chosen:

$$\frac{\pi\,(2\,\epsilon)^2}{\pi\,\rho^2} \;=\; \frac{4\,\epsilon^2}{\rho^2} \;\;.$$

Since the model points are chosen independently, the expected number of points confusable with a random point $\mathbf{p}_i$ equals $(n-1)$ times the probability that a single point (such as $\mathbf{p}_j$ above) is confusable with it. We therefore have an upper bound on E_C, the expected number of points confusable with a given point:

$$E_C \;\leqslant\; (n-1)\,\frac{4\,\epsilon^2}{\rho^2} \;\;.$$

If $\rho \;\geqslant\; 2\epsilon\sqrt{n/\kappa}$, this becomes

$$E_C \;\leqslant\; \frac{4\,(n-1)\,\epsilon^2}{4\,\epsilon^2\,(n/\kappa)} \;=\; \frac{(n-1)\,\kappa}{n} \;\leqslant\; \kappa \quad \blacksquare$$

To strengthen the reader's intuition that this is a reasonable way to control the asymptotic effects of noise, we point out an alternative argument that leads to the same relation. The *total* area of all the noise polygons is bounded from above by

$$\sum_{i=1}^{n}(\,\pi\,\epsilon^2\,) \;=\; n\,\pi\,\epsilon^2 \;\;.$$

If the ratio of this sum to the area $\pi\rho^2$ of the model is not bounded, then with increasing n the total effects of noise clearly grow disproportionately. If there is an upper bound on this ratio, say κ', we have the relation $\dfrac{n\,\pi\,\epsilon^2}{\pi\,\rho^2} \;\leqslant\; \kappa'$ and thus the familiar form: $\rho \;\geqslant\; \epsilon\sqrt{n/\kappa'}$.

This policy is illustrated in Figure 7-4, using fixed ρ and κ, and thus varying ϵ, for the cases $n = 9$ and $n = 36$ (the upper limit of the Monte Carlo trials reported later in Chapter 10).

To summarize, we have derived an expression relating the scale of the model pattern to worst-case noise that will guarantee any given bound κ on the expected number of points confusable with a random model point. This is done to ensure that the effects of noise are comparable among patterns of different sizes, permitting meaningful asymptotic analysis.

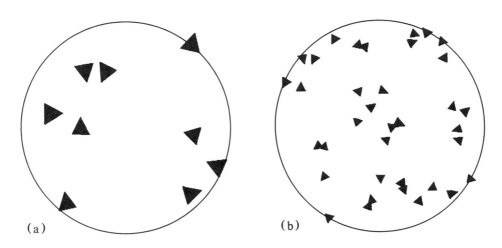

Figure 7 - 4. Random models generated using the same κ and ρ: (a) $n = 9$; and
(b) $n = 36$.

From this point on, when describing random patterns of size n, *generated using* κ and ϵ, we will assume that the scale of the model ρ is computed using $\rho = 2 \epsilon \sqrt{n/\kappa}$.

We have not yet pinned down what we mean by "moderate" noise since we have not yet chosen bounds on κ. This will done in Chapter 9, after we consider the effects of noise on expected ellipsoid geometry.

7.3. Geometric Probability for Random Patterns

We first develop some simple upper bounds on the expected fraction of points falling within randomly-located "probe" circles.

Lemma 7-2. For random P generated using ρ, any fixed subset $P' \subseteq P$, and a random point $\tilde{\mathbf{p}}$ (not necessarily in P), distributed independently of P' (but otherwise arbitrarily), the expected fraction of points of P' falling inside a circle centered at $\tilde{\mathbf{p}}$ of radius δ is at most $\left(\dfrac{\delta}{\rho} \right)^2$.

Proof. If the probe circle — call it C_P — lies entirely within the generating circle, then the expected fraction of P' falling inside C_P is simply the ratio of areas

$$\frac{\pi \, \delta^2}{\pi \, \rho^2} \;=\; \left(\frac{\delta}{\rho} \right)^2 .$$

This holds due to the independence of $\tilde{\mathbf{p}}$ and P' and the uniform distribution of the points of P' within the generating circle.

If C_P falls partly or wholly outside the generating circle, the expected fraction will be smaller than above, since the density functions of the points of P' are zero outside the generating circle. ∎

Lemma 7-3. For random P and Q generated using ϵ, ρ, $\hat{M}$, and $\hat{\mathbf{R}}$, any fixed subset $Q' \subseteq Q$, and a random point $\tilde{\mathbf{q}}$ (not necessarily in Q), distributed independently of Q' (and otherwise arbitrarily), the expected fraction of points of Q' falling within a circle centered at $\tilde{\mathbf{q}}$ of radius δ is at most $\left(\dfrac{\delta \hat{r}_s + \epsilon}{\rho} \right)^2$ (recall that $\hat{r}_s$ is the scale factor $\| \hat{\mathbf{r}}_{12} \|$ of $\hat{\mathbf{R}}$).

Proof. Let $P' \equiv \{ \mathbf{p} \mid (\exists \mathbf{q} \in Q) \; \hat{M}(\mathbf{p}) = \mathbf{q} \}$, and note that $|P'| = |Q'|$. For each $\mathbf{q} \in Q'$ that falls within the probe circle — call it C_Q — then $\mathbf{p} = \hat{M}^{-1}(\mathbf{q})$ is located so that $\| \hat{\mathbf{R}}(\mathbf{q}) - \mathbf{p} \| \leqslant \epsilon$: thus this $\mathbf{p}$ falls within a circle — call it C_P — centered at $\tilde{\mathbf{p}} \equiv \hat{\mathbf{R}}(\tilde{\mathbf{q}})$, of radius $\delta_P = \delta \hat{r}_s + \epsilon$. Thus, the fraction of Q' falling within C_Q is at most the fraction of P' falling within C_P.

Now, since random $\tilde{\mathbf{q}}$ is distributed independently of Q', $\tilde{\mathbf{p}}$, which depends only on $\tilde{\mathbf{q}}$ and $\hat{\mathbf{R}}$ (which is fixed), must be distributed independently of P'. Thus we can apply Lemma 7-2 to conclude that the expected fraction of points of Q' falling within the probe circle C_Q is at most $\left(\dfrac{\delta \hat{r}_s + \epsilon}{\rho} \right)^2$. ∎

We review some results of geometric probability, concerning points chosen at random uniformly within a circle.

Lemma 7-4. For random P generated using ρ, let random variable $D_i = \| \mathbf{p}_i \|$, the distance from the origin of the ith model point. Then, the probability density function of D_i, for any $i = 1,...,n$, is

$$f_{D_i}(d) = \frac{2d}{\rho^2} \tag{7-1}$$

and

$$E[D_i] = \frac{2}{3}\rho \quad \text{and} \quad Var[D_i] = \frac{\rho^2}{18} \tag{7-2}$$

Further, let random variable $D_{\max} = \max\limits_{i=1,...,n} \{D_i\}$, the farthest distance of any point of P from the origin; then

$$f_{D_{\max}}(d) = \frac{2n}{\rho^{2n}} d^{2n-1} \quad \text{and} \quad E[D_{\max}] = \frac{n}{n + \frac{1}{2}}\rho \tag{7-3}$$

For all $i = 1,...,n$, and for random model point $\mathbf{p}_i = (x_i, y_i)^T$, the random variables $X_i = x_i$ and $Y_i = y_i$ are identically distributed with density

$$f_{X_i}(d) = f_{Y_i}(d) = \frac{2}{\pi} \frac{\sqrt{\rho^2 - d^2}}{\rho^2} , \tag{7-4}$$

mean $E[X_i] = E[Y_i] = 0$, and variance $Var[X_i] = Var[Y_i] = \dfrac{\rho^2}{4}$.

Proof. These are well-known, elementary results of geometric probability; see [27] for derivations. ∎

We can use these to find an upper bound on the expected distance of P's centroid from the origin.

Lemma   7-5.   Let $\bar{\mathbf{p}} = \dfrac{1}{n}\sum\limits_{i=1}^{n}\mathbf{p}_i;$ then, $E[\bar{\mathbf{p}}] = \begin{pmatrix} 0 \\ 0 \end{pmatrix}$ and

$E[\,\|\bar{\mathbf{p}}\|\,] \leqslant \dfrac{\rho}{\sqrt{2\,n}}.$

Proof. Let random variables $\bar{X} = \dfrac{1}{n}\sum\limits_{i=1}^{n}x_i$ and $\bar{Y} = \dfrac{1}{n}\sum\limits_{i=1}^{n}y_i.$ Note that

$$E[\bar{X}] = \frac{1}{n}\sum_{i=1}^{n}E[x_i] = 0$$

since each $E[x_i] = 0$. A parallel argument gives $E[\bar{Y}] = 0$. Thus,

$$E[\bar{\mathbf{p}}] = \begin{bmatrix} E[\bar{X}] \\ E[\bar{Y}] \end{bmatrix} = \begin{pmatrix} 0 \\ 0 \end{pmatrix}.$$

Now, $\|\bar{\mathbf{p}}\| = \sqrt{\bar{X}^2 + \bar{Y}^2}$. Since $\sqrt{\cdot}$ is a concave function, by Jensen's inequality we have $E[\,\|\bar{\mathbf{p}}\|\,] \leqslant \sqrt{E[\bar{X}^2] + E[\bar{Y}^2]}$.

Now, by Lemma 7-4, for any $i = 1,...,n$, random variables X_i and Y_i are identically distributed, so $E[\,\|\bar{\mathbf{p}}\|\,] \leqslant \sqrt{2E[\bar{X}^2]}$. Also, the set of random variables $\{X_i/n\}_{i=1,...,n}$ is independent (by definition of a random model), and have common mean $\mu = 0$ and variance $\rho^2/(4\,n^2)$, by Lemma 7-4. Thus,

$$Var[\bar{X}] = \sum_{i=1}^{n}\frac{\rho^2}{4\,n^2} = \frac{\rho^2}{4\,n}$$

Now, again using the independence of $\{X_i\}_{i=1,...,n}$, we know that $Var[\bar{X}] = E[\bar{X}^2] - E[\bar{X}]^2 = E[\bar{X}^2]$. Thus, $E[\bar{X}^2] = \rho^2/4\,n$, and so

$$E[\,\|\bar{\mathbf{p}}\|\,] \leqslant \sqrt{2\rho^2/4\,n} = \frac{\rho}{\sqrt{2\,n}} \quad \blacksquare$$

Recall that during the generation of Q, for each $\mathbf{p}_i$, a random noise vector $\hat{\boldsymbol{\epsilon}}_i$ was chosen uniformly within $\mathbf{p}_i$'s noise polygon. The distribution of this noise vector is analyzed next.

Lemma 7-6. For random P and Q, generated using l_{max}, ϵ, and noise vectors $\{\hat{\boldsymbol{\epsilon}}_i\}_{i=1,...,n}$; for each $i = 1,...,n$, let random variable $\hat{C}_i$ denote the shortest distance of $\mathbf{p}_i + \hat{\boldsymbol{\epsilon}}_i$ to the sides of the noise polygon for $\mathbf{p}_i$; then the probability density function for $\hat{C}_i$ is

$$f_{\hat{C}_i}(c) \;\; = \;\; \frac{2}{H^2}\,(H-c) \tag{7-7}$$

where $H = \epsilon \cos(\dfrac{\pi}{l_{max}})$; and

$$E[\hat{C}_i] \;\; = \;\; \frac{H}{3} \;\; . \tag{7-8}$$

Also, let random variable $\hat{C}_{min} \equiv \min_{i=1,...,n} \{\hat{C}_i\}$; then its p.d.f. is

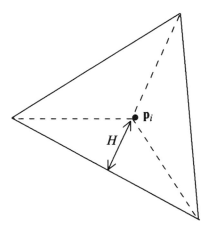

Figure 7 - 5.   A random noise polygon, partitioned.

$$f\hat{C}_{min}(c) = \frac{2n}{H^{2n}}(H - c)^{2n-1} \tag{7-9}$$

and

$$E[\hat{C}_{min}] = \frac{H}{2n+1} \quad . \tag{7-10}$$

Proof. The distributions of $\hat{C}_i$ are identical for all i, since the polygons differ only in their rotation angle about the origin. The vector $\mathbf{p}_i + \hat{\boldsymbol{\epsilon}}_i$ is farthest from all sides when, of course, it coincides with $\mathbf{p}_i$, and this distance is H defined above (see Figure 7-5).

Partition a noise polygon as follows: draw lines from $\mathbf{p}_i$ to the l_{max} vertices, forming congruent isosceles triangles. Now, random $\mathbf{p}_i + \hat{\boldsymbol{\epsilon}}_i$ falls in exactly one of these with probability 1, and it is closer to the exterior side of that triangle than any other side of the polygon. So $\hat{C}_i$ is distributed as the distance to this exterior side from a point chosen uniformly within the triangle. It is easy to show that this density is as given in equation (7-7). The assumption of independence among the $\{\hat{\boldsymbol{\epsilon}}_i\}_{i=1,...,n}$ can be used to develop (7-9). ∎

7.4. Geometry of Feasible Regions

We now approach a generalization of Lemma 5-1: just as two pairs of matched points determine a *unique* feasible registration when $\epsilon = 0$, they also determine a *bounded set* of feasible registrations when $\epsilon \geqslant 0$. First, we show how to isolate analytically the effects of model noise on registrations.

Theorem 7-1. For any model P and instance Q, any k-matching M, $k \geqslant 2$, and any two distinct matched points $\mathbf{q}_a = M(\mathbf{p}_a)$ and $\mathbf{q}_b = M(\mathbf{p}_b)$, every registration $\mathbf{R}$ can be written as $\tilde{\mathbf{R}} + \delta\mathbf{R}$, where

$$\tilde{\mathbf{R}} \;=\; \begin{bmatrix} \bar{\mathbf{p}} - \dfrac{\Delta\mathbf{p}}{\Delta\mathbf{q}}\,\bar{\mathbf{q}} \\[2ex] \dfrac{\Delta\mathbf{p}}{\Delta\mathbf{q}} \end{bmatrix} \qquad \text{and} \qquad \delta\mathbf{R} \;=\; \begin{bmatrix} \bar{\boldsymbol{\epsilon}} - \dfrac{\Delta\boldsymbol{\epsilon}}{\Delta\mathbf{q}}\,\bar{\mathbf{q}} \\[2ex] \dfrac{\Delta\boldsymbol{\epsilon}}{\Delta\mathbf{q}} \end{bmatrix}$$

where $\bar{\mathbf{p}} \equiv (\mathbf{p}_a + \mathbf{p}_b)/2$, $\Delta\mathbf{p} \equiv \mathbf{p}_b - \mathbf{p}_a$, and $\bar{\mathbf{q}}$ and $\Delta\mathbf{q}$ are defined analogously; similarly, $\bar{\boldsymbol{\epsilon}}$ and $\Delta\boldsymbol{\epsilon}$ are defined using $\boldsymbol{\epsilon}_a \equiv \mathbf{R}(\mathbf{q}_a) - \mathbf{p}_a$ and $\boldsymbol{\epsilon}_b \equiv \mathbf{R}(\mathbf{q}_b) - \mathbf{p}_b$.

Proof. By substitution:

$$\tilde{\mathbf{R}} + \delta\mathbf{R} \;=\; \begin{bmatrix} (\bar{\mathbf{p}} - \dfrac{\Delta\mathbf{p}}{\Delta\mathbf{q}}\,\bar{\mathbf{q}}) + (\bar{\boldsymbol{\epsilon}} - \dfrac{\Delta\boldsymbol{\epsilon}}{\Delta\mathbf{q}}\,\bar{\mathbf{q}}) \\[2ex] \dfrac{\Delta\mathbf{p}}{\Delta\mathbf{q}} + \dfrac{\Delta\boldsymbol{\epsilon}}{\Delta\mathbf{q}} \end{bmatrix}$$

$$=\; \begin{bmatrix} \bar{\mathbf{p}} + \bar{\boldsymbol{\epsilon}} - \dfrac{\Delta\mathbf{p} + \Delta\boldsymbol{\epsilon}}{\Delta\mathbf{q}}\,\bar{\mathbf{q}} \\[2ex] \dfrac{\Delta\mathbf{p} + \Delta\boldsymbol{\epsilon}}{\Delta\mathbf{q}} \end{bmatrix} \qquad\qquad (7\text{-}11)$$

Now, $\bar{\mathbf{p}} + \bar{\boldsymbol{\epsilon}} = \tfrac{1}{2}(\mathbf{p}_a + \mathbf{p}_b) + \tfrac{1}{2}(\boldsymbol{\epsilon}_a + \boldsymbol{\epsilon}_b) = \tfrac{1}{2}(\mathbf{p}_a + \mathbf{p}_b + \mathbf{R}(\mathbf{q}_a) - \mathbf{p}_a + \mathbf{R}(\mathbf{q}_b) - \mathbf{p}_b) = \tfrac{1}{2}(\mathbf{R}(\mathbf{q}_a) + \mathbf{R}(\mathbf{q}_b)) = \mathbf{R}(\bar{\mathbf{q}}) = \mathbf{r}_{xy} + \mathbf{r}_{12}\,\bar{\mathbf{q}}$. Also, $\Delta\mathbf{p} + \Delta\boldsymbol{\epsilon} = (\mathbf{p}_b - \mathbf{p}_a) + (\boldsymbol{\epsilon}_b - \boldsymbol{\epsilon}_a) = \mathbf{p}_b - \mathbf{p}_a + \mathbf{R}(\mathbf{q}_b) - \mathbf{p}_b - \mathbf{R}(\mathbf{q}_a) + \mathbf{p}_a = \mathbf{R}(\mathbf{q}_b) - \mathbf{R}(\mathbf{q}_a) = \mathbf{r}_{12}(\mathbf{q}_b - \mathbf{q}_a) = \mathbf{r}_{12}\,\Delta\mathbf{q}$. Substituting these results into equation (7-11) gives

$$\tilde{\mathbf{R}} + \delta\mathbf{R} \;=\; \begin{bmatrix} \mathbf{r}_{xy} + \mathbf{r}_{12}\,\bar{\mathbf{q}} - \dfrac{\mathbf{r}_{12}\,\Delta\mathbf{q}}{\Delta\mathbf{q}}\,\bar{\mathbf{q}} \\[2ex] \dfrac{\mathbf{r}_{12}\,\Delta\mathbf{q}}{\Delta\mathbf{q}} \end{bmatrix} \;=\; \begin{bmatrix} \mathbf{r}_{xy} \\[1ex] \mathbf{r}_{12} \end{bmatrix} \;=\; \mathbf{R} \quad \blacksquare$$

Note that the degenerate case $\boldsymbol{\epsilon}_a = \boldsymbol{\epsilon}_b = (0,0)^T$ gives the result of Lemma 5-1. Now we apply the theorem to the case of feasible matchings, and prove that the set of feasible registrations is bounded.

Corollary 7-1. For random P and Q generated using $\boldsymbol{\epsilon}$, any feasible k-matching M, $k \geqslant 2$, and any two pairs of distinct matched points $\mathbf{q}_a = M(\mathbf{p}_a)$

and $\mathbf{q}_b = M(\mathbf{p}_b)$, there is a fixed $\tilde{\mathbf{R}}$ such that every feasible registration $\mathbf{R}$ may be written as $\tilde{\mathbf{R}} + \delta\mathbf{R}$, and $\delta\mathbf{R}$ is bounded as follows:

$$\|\delta\mathbf{r}_{xy}\| \quad \leqslant \quad \left(1 + \frac{2\|\bar{\mathbf{q}}\|}{\|\Delta\mathbf{q}\|}\right)\epsilon \qquad \text{and} \qquad \|\delta\mathbf{r}_{12}\| \quad \leqslant \quad \left(\frac{2}{\|\Delta\mathbf{q}\|}\right)\epsilon$$

where $\bar{\mathbf{q}} \equiv (\mathbf{q}_a + \mathbf{q}_b)/2$, and $\Delta\mathbf{q} \equiv \mathbf{q}_b - \mathbf{q}_a$.

Proof. Define $\bar{\mathbf{p}}$, $\Delta\mathbf{p}$, ϵ_a, ϵ_b, $\bar{\epsilon}$, and $\Delta\epsilon$ as in Theorem 7-1. Also, choose $\tilde{\mathbf{R}}$ and $\delta\mathbf{R}$ to be the ones derived in the Theorem. Now, for any feasible registration $\mathbf{R}$ under M, the noisy images of $\mathbf{p}_a$ and $\mathbf{p}_b$ ($\mathbf{R}(M(\mathbf{p}_a))$ and $\mathbf{R}(M(\mathbf{p}_b))$) must satisfy the noise constraints for $\mathbf{p}_a$ and $\mathbf{p}_b$. This implies $\|\mathbf{R}(M(\mathbf{p}_a)) - \mathbf{p}_a\| \leqslant \epsilon$ and $\|\mathbf{R}(M(\mathbf{p}_b)) - \mathbf{p}_b\| \leqslant \epsilon$, which is the same as $\|\epsilon_a\| \leqslant \epsilon$ and $\|\epsilon_b\| \leqslant \epsilon$. Clearly, this implies $\|\bar{\epsilon}\| \leqslant \epsilon$ and $\|\Delta\epsilon\| \leqslant 2\epsilon$. From the Theorem we have

$$\|\delta\mathbf{r}_{xy}\| \quad = \quad \|\bar{\epsilon} - \frac{\Delta\epsilon}{\Delta\mathbf{q}}\bar{\mathbf{q}}\| \quad \leqslant \quad \|\bar{\epsilon}\| + \frac{\|\Delta\epsilon\|}{\|\Delta\mathbf{q}\|}\|\bar{\mathbf{q}}\|$$

$$\leqslant \quad \epsilon + \frac{\|\bar{\mathbf{q}}\|}{\|\Delta\mathbf{q}\|}(2\epsilon) \quad = \quad \left(1 + \frac{2\|\bar{\mathbf{q}}\|}{\|\Delta\mathbf{q}\|}\right)\epsilon$$

$$\|\delta\mathbf{r}_{12}\| \quad = \quad \frac{\|\Delta\epsilon\|}{\|\Delta\mathbf{q}\|} \quad \leqslant \quad \left(\frac{2}{\|\Delta\mathbf{q}\|}\right)\epsilon \quad \blacksquare$$

We can use Corollary 7-1 to place an upper bound on the volume of the set of feasible registrations.

Corollary 7-2. For random P and Q generated using ϵ, any feasible k-matching M, $k \geqslant 2$, and any two distinct matched instance points $\mathbf{q}_a$ and $\mathbf{q}_b$, all feasible registrations are contained in an ellipsoid whose volume is bounded above by

$$\frac{8\pi^2}{3} \frac{(\|\Delta\mathbf{q}\| + 2\|\bar{\mathbf{q}}\|)^2}{\|\Delta\mathbf{q}\|^4}\epsilon^4$$

where $\Delta\mathbf{q} \equiv \mathbf{q}_b - \mathbf{q}_a$, and $\bar{\mathbf{q}} \equiv (\mathbf{q}_a + \mathbf{q}_b)/2$.

Proof. Let the center of the ellipsoid be $\widetilde{\mathbf{R}}$, and the bounds on $\|\delta\mathbf{r}_{xy}\|$ and $\|\delta\mathbf{r}_{12}\|$ be as given in Corollary 7-1. Then, by the results of Section 5.4, we can construct an ellipsoid enforcing these bounds with volume at most

$$\frac{2\pi^2}{3}\left[\left(1+\frac{2\|\overline{\mathbf{q}}\|}{\|\Delta\mathbf{q}\|}\right)\epsilon\right]^2\left[\left(\frac{2}{\|\Delta\mathbf{q}\|}\right)\epsilon\right]^2$$

which simplifies to the result. $\blacksquare$

7.5. Prior Constraint Strategies

As we saw in Section 6.2, we can exploit the absence of spurious and missing points to apply constraints on feasible registrations prior to matching any points. We will explore the results of applying two such prior constraint strategies to random patterns.

The first is the technique of "matched-centroids", in which both model and instance patterns are translated so that their centroids are at the origin. Also, the two origin points are treated as special extra pattern points which are permanently matched.

The second we call the "farthest-first" strategy, in which the farthest model point from the origin is selected as the first model point (after the centroid) to be matched.

7.5.1. Matched-centroids strategy

In Section 6.2.1, we saw that translation could be bounded by computing the centroids $\overline{\mathbf{p}}$ and $\overline{\mathbf{q}}$ in $O(n)$ time, then treating them as special points in each pattern, which are permanently matched. Since the magnitude of the noise constraints on $\overline{\mathbf{p}}$ obey the same upper bound ϵ as the other points, the corollaries of Theorem 7-1 apply also to these special points.

As a part of the strategy, we also translate each pattern so that its centroid is at the origin, in $O(n)$ time. This will have no effect on the matchings found, and the pointwise noise constraints also are unaffected.

The effect of this preprocessing on P and Q will be denoted P^+ and Q^+, where

$$P^+ \equiv\ <\mathbf{p}_i^+>_{i=0,1,\ldots,n} \qquad\qquad Q^+ \equiv\ <\mathbf{q}_j^+>_{j=0,1,\ldots,n}$$

$$\mathbf{p}_0^+ \equiv (0,0)^T \qquad\qquad\qquad \mathbf{q}_0^+ \equiv (0,0)^T$$

$$\mathbf{p}_i^+ \equiv \mathbf{p}_i - \bar{\mathbf{p}}, \quad i=1,\ldots,n \qquad \mathbf{q}_j^+ \equiv \mathbf{q}_j - \bar{\mathbf{q}}, \quad j=1,\ldots,n$$

Given any M defined for P and Q, we define M^+ for P^+ and Q^+ in the obvious way: if $M(\mathbf{p}_i) = \mathbf{q}_j$, then $M^+(\mathbf{p}_i^+) \equiv \mathbf{q}_j^+$.

There are simple mappings from untranslated to translated registrations, and back again:

Lemma 7-7. If $\mathbf{R}$ is feasible for P, Q, and M, then

$$\mathbf{R}^+ = \begin{pmatrix} \mathbf{R}(\bar{\mathbf{q}}) - \bar{\mathbf{p}} \\ \mathbf{r}_{12} \end{pmatrix}$$

is feasible for P^+, Q^+, and M^+. Back the other way: if $\mathbf{R}^+$ is feasible for P^+, Q^+, and M^+, then

$$\mathbf{R} = \begin{pmatrix} \bar{\mathbf{p}} + \mathbf{R}^+(-\bar{\mathbf{q}}) \\ \mathbf{r}_{12}^+ \end{pmatrix}$$

is feasible for P, Q and M. Also, if $\mathbf{R}^+$ and $\mathbf{R}$ correspond in this way, they produce identical noise vectors, *i.e.*, for all $i, j = 1,\ldots,n$, $\mathbf{R}(\mathbf{q}_j) - \mathbf{p}_i = \mathbf{R}^+(\mathbf{q}_j^+) - \mathbf{p}_i^+$.

Proof. By substitution. ∎

Now we fulfill a promise made in a footnote in Section 6.2.1, by showing that matching centroids has the effect of bounding feasible translations.

Lemma 7-8. For random P and Q generated using ϵ, $\hat{M}$, and $\hat{\mathbf{R}}$, after matching centroids, $\| \hat{\mathbf{r}}_{xy}^+ \| \leq \epsilon$.

Proof. By the analysis of Section 6.2.1 (Equation 6-6), we know that for any feasible total matching, any resulting noise vector of the centroid $\bar{\epsilon}$ obeys the magnitude bound $\| \bar{\epsilon} \| \leqslant \epsilon$. In particular, $\hat{M}^+$ is a total feasible matching, and by the matched-centroids strategy, $\hat{M}^+(\mathbf{p}_0^+) = \mathbf{q}_0^+$. Thus, the noise vector $\epsilon_0 \equiv \hat{R}^+(\mathbf{q}_0^+) - \mathbf{p}_0^+$ obeys the bound. But,

$$\hat{R}^+(\mathbf{q}_0^+) - \mathbf{p}_0^+ = \hat{R}^+\left(\begin{pmatrix} 0 \\ 0 \end{pmatrix} \right) - \begin{pmatrix} 0 \\ 0 \end{pmatrix} = \hat{r}_{xy}^+ ,$$

since $\mathbf{p}_0^+$ and $\mathbf{q}_0^+$ are translated to the origin. Thus, $\| \hat{r}_{xy}^+ \| = \| \epsilon_0 \| \leqslant \epsilon$. ∎

Under the matched-centroids strategy, the computation of upper bounds on the volume of the feasible set is simplified.

Lemma 7-9. For random P, Q, generated using ϵ, any feasible k-matching M, $k \geqslant 1$, and any matched pair $M(\mathbf{p}_a) = \mathbf{q}_a$, after matching centroids we can construct an ellipsoid containing all feasible registrations whose volume is no more than

$$\frac{32\pi^2}{3} \frac{\epsilon^4}{\| \mathbf{q}_a^+ \|^2} .$$

Proof. Applying Corollary 7-2 to this case, identify the Corollary's $\mathbf{p}_a$ with this case's $\mathbf{p}_0^+$, $\mathbf{q}_a$ with $\mathbf{q}_0^+$, $\mathbf{p}_b$ with $\mathbf{p}_a^+$, and $\mathbf{q}_b$ with $\mathbf{q}_a^+$. Since $\mathbf{q}_0^+$ is the origin, there are simplifications: the Corollary's $\Delta \mathbf{q} = (0,0)^T - \mathbf{q}_a^+ = -\mathbf{q}_a^+$, and its $\bar{\mathbf{q}} = ((0,0)^T + \mathbf{q}_a^+)/2 = \mathbf{q}_a^+/2$. Thus, the upper bound on ellipsoid volume becomes

$$\frac{8\pi^2}{3} \frac{\left[\| \mathbf{q}_a^+ \| + 2 \left(\frac{\| \mathbf{q}_a^+ \|}{2} \right) \right]^2}{\| \mathbf{q}_a^+ \|^4} \epsilon^4$$

which simplifies to the result. ∎

7.5.2. Farthest-first strategy

A second strategy, in combination with matched-centroids, will help us place tight bounds (both upper and lower) on the volume of feasible regions: this is a "farthest-first" policy, in which comparison order among model points is chosen so that the first model point to be matched, $\mathbf{p}_1^+$, is the farthest from the (translated) origin.

We use the notation $\rho_i \equiv \| \mathbf{p}_i^+ \|$ and $\rho_{max} \equiv \| \mathbf{p}_1^+ \| = \max_{i=1,\dots,n} \{ \rho_i \}$. We can place bounds on $E[\rho_i]$ and $E[\rho_{max}]$:

Lemma 7-10. For random P, Q, generated using fixed κ and ϵ, after matched-centroids and farthest-first preprocessing, we have the bounds

$$\left[\frac{4\sqrt{n}}{3} - \sqrt{2} \right] \frac{\epsilon}{\sqrt{\kappa}} \;\leqslant\; E[\rho_i] \;\leqslant\; \left[\frac{4\sqrt{n}}{3} + \sqrt{2} \right] \frac{\epsilon}{\sqrt{\kappa}}$$

$$\left[\frac{2n\sqrt{n}}{n + \frac{1}{2}} - \sqrt{2} \right] \frac{\epsilon}{\sqrt{\kappa}} \;\leqslant\; E[\rho_{max}] \;\leqslant\; \left[\frac{2n\sqrt{n}}{n + \frac{1}{2}} + \sqrt{2} \right] \frac{\epsilon}{\sqrt{\kappa}}$$

Proof. By definition $\rho_i = \| \mathbf{p}_i^+ \| = \| \mathbf{p}_i - \bar{\mathbf{p}} \| \geqslant \| \mathbf{p}_i \| - \| \bar{\mathbf{p}} \|$. Thus $E[\rho_i] \geqslant E[\| \mathbf{p}_i \|] - E[\| \bar{\mathbf{p}} \|]$; by Lemma 7-4, $E[\| \mathbf{p}_i \|] = 2\rho/3$, so $E[\rho_i] \geqslant (2\rho/3) - E[\| \bar{\mathbf{p}} \|]$. Now, by Lemma 7-5, $E[\| \bar{\mathbf{p}} \|] \leqslant \rho/\sqrt{2n}$, so

$$E[\rho_i] \;\geqslant\; \frac{2}{3}\rho - \frac{\rho}{\sqrt{2n}} \;=\; \left[\frac{2}{3} - \frac{1}{\sqrt{2n}} \right] \rho \quad .$$

But recall that $\rho \equiv 2\epsilon\sqrt{n}/\kappa$ by definition, so

$$E[\rho_i] \;\geqslant\; \left[\frac{4}{3}\sqrt{n} - \frac{2\sqrt{n}}{\sqrt{2n}} \right] \frac{\epsilon}{\sqrt{\kappa}}$$

$$=\; \left[\frac{4\sqrt{n}}{3} - \sqrt{2} \right] \frac{\epsilon}{\sqrt{\kappa}} \quad .$$

The upper bound for $E[\rho_i]$ is derived similarly starting with $\| \mathbf{p}_i - \bar{\mathbf{p}} \| \leqslant$

$\| \mathbf{p}_i \| + \| \bar{\mathbf{p}} \|$. A parallel pair of arguments, using equation (7-3) from Lemma 7-4, gives the results for $E[\rho_{max}]$. ▮

CHAPTER 8

Expected Cost
of Feasibility Testing

We can now prove an asymptotic upper bound on the expected number of ellipsoid contractions along a special long path in the search tree. Although we do not have a complete analysis of the *total* expected number of contractions throughout the tree, this proven bound is encouragingly low: $O(\log n)$.

8.1. Number of Ellipsoid Contractions

Consider the operation of the algorithm as it tests the feasibility of a specific total matching M. We begin by testing its "1-prefix" M_1 (the matching of size 1 that is a prefix of M), and, if it is feasible, we proceed to test each k-prefix M_k in turn until proven infeasible or $k = n$, in which case M is a successful matching. The 1-prefix of any matching defines a bounded feasible region (unless, with probability 0, $M_1(\mathbf{p}_1^{\dagger}) = (0,0)^T$, in which case the feasible region is unbounded). Using a matched-centroids strategy, we can compute an ellipsoid enclosing the region. Let us call the initial feasible region $\mathbf{F}_1$ and the initial ellipsoid $\mathbf{E}_1$.

When M_k is tested $(k > 1)$, additional constraints may reduce the feasible set (from $\mathbf{F}_{k-1}$ to $\mathbf{F}_k$). As a result, the prior ellipsoid $\mathbf{E}_{k-1}$ may undergo contractions, as the Soviet ellipsoid algorithm attempts to find a new feasible center. If successful, the result is a new ellipsoid $\mathbf{E}_k$; if not, the prior ellipsoid shrinks until it is entirely excluded by some constraint, and so vanishes. At all times, the current ellipsoid contains all feasible registrations, so $Vol(\mathbf{E}_k) \geqslant Vol(\mathbf{F}_k)$.

Our strategy is simply to bound the volume of the initial ellipsoid, $Vol(\mathbf{E}_1)$, from above (by, say, B_1), and bound the volume of the final feasible set, $Vol(\mathbf{F}_k)$, from below (by, say, B_k). Each contraction, as we have seen in Section 4.3.2, shrinks volume by at least the constant factor $\sigma \approx 0.905$. Thus the number of contractions required to prove M_k feasible will be bounded above by the log-ratio

$$\log_\sigma \left[\frac{B_1}{B_k} \right] \quad .$$

(If, however, M_k is *infeasible*, then this approach does not work, since the "final" volume is zero. We have not found a good way to analyze this case.)

8.2. The Search Path to $\hat{M}$

Among all the search paths in the (pruned) search tree, only the path to $\hat{M}$ is guaranteed to remain feasible for all $k = 1,..,n$ (see Figure 8-1). We will apply the strategy described above to this interesting case, and begin with a Lemma which will help place an upper bound on $Vol(\mathbf{E}_1)$ for $\hat{M}$.

Lemma 8-1. For random P, Q, generated using κ, ϵ, $\hat{\mathbf{R}}$, and $\hat{M}$, after matched-centroids and farthest-first preprocessing, we can construct an initial ellipsoid $\mathbf{E}_1$ (containing all feasible registrations) whose volume is no more than

$$\frac{32\pi^2}{3} \frac{\epsilon^4 \hat{r}_s^2}{(\rho_{max} - 2\epsilon)^2} \quad .$$

Proof. We will apply Lemmas 7-7, 7-8, and 7-9: identify the $\mathbf{q}_a^+$ of Lemma 7-9 with $\hat{M}^+(\mathbf{p}_1^+)$; then, $\| \mathbf{q}_a^+ \| = \| (\hat{\mathbf{R}}^+)^{-1}(\mathbf{p}_1^+ + \epsilon_1) \|$, for some noise vector ϵ_1 obeying $\| \epsilon_1 \| \leqslant \epsilon$. Now,

$$(\hat{\mathbf{R}}^+)^{-1}(\mathbf{p}_1^+ + \epsilon_1) = \frac{(\mathbf{p}_1^+ + \epsilon_1) - \hat{\mathbf{r}}_{xy}^+}{\hat{\mathbf{r}}_{12}^+} = \frac{\mathbf{p}_1^+ + \epsilon_1 - \hat{\mathbf{r}}_{xy}^+}{\hat{\mathbf{r}}_{12}}$$

since, by Lemma 7-7, $\hat{\mathbf{r}}_{12}^+ = \hat{\mathbf{r}}_{12}$. Taking magnitudes, we have

$$\| \mathbf{q}_a^+ \| \geqslant \frac{\| \mathbf{p}_1^+ \| - \| \epsilon_1 \| - \| \hat{\mathbf{r}}_{xy}^+ \|}{\| \hat{\mathbf{r}}_{12} \|} = \frac{\rho_{max} - \| \epsilon_1 \| - \| \hat{\mathbf{r}}_{xy}^+ \|}{\hat{r}_s}$$

using the farthest-first strategy of selecting $\mathbf{p}_1^+$, and the definition of $\hat{r}_s$. From

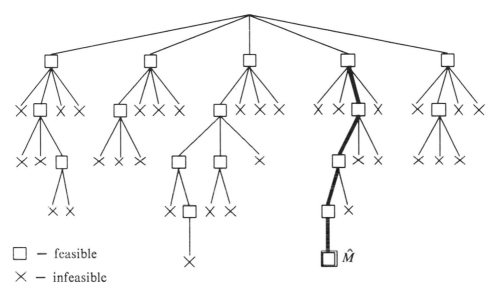

Figure 8 - 1.   The search path to $\hat{M}$.

Lemma 7-8, we know that $\| \hat{\mathbf{r}}_{xy}^+ \| \leqslant \epsilon$, so finally $\| \mathbf{q}_a^+ \| \geqslant (\rho_{max} - 2\epsilon) / \hat{r}_s$. Substituting this bound in the result of Lemma 7-9 gives the result. $\blacksquare$

Note that the initial ellipsoid can be explicitly constructed using details of the proofs of Corollary 7-2 and Lemma 7-9. Next, we will develop a result that will help place lower bounds on the expected volume of the final feasible region $Vol(\mathbf{F}_n)$.

Lemma 8-2. For random P, Q, generated using κ, ϵ, $\{\hat{\epsilon}_i\}_{i-1,...,n}$, $\hat{\mathbf{R}}$, and $\hat{M}$, and any matched pair $\hat{M}(\mathbf{p}_i) = \mathbf{q}_j$, after matched-centroid and farthest-first preprocessing, the closest approach c_i^+ of the corresponding registration constraint hyperplanes to $\hat{\mathbf{R}}^+$ is bounded below, as follows:

$$c_i^+ \;\geqslant\; \frac{\hat{c}_i\,\hat{r}_s}{\rho_{max} + \epsilon + \hat{r}_s}$$

where $\hat{c}_i$ is the closest approach of noise vector $\hat{\epsilon}_i$ to the sides of the noise polygon for model point $\mathbf{p}_i$.

Proof. Let $< \mathbf{U}_i, \mathbf{d}_i >$ be the set of noise contraints for $\mathbf{p}_i$. We will apply Lemma 5-3 to each constraint $< \mathbf{u}_{ik}, d_{ik} >$, $k = 1,...,l_{max}$: the (signed) closest approach distance of the corresponding registration constraint hyperplane to $\hat{\mathbf{R}}^+$ is given by

$$\frac{d_{ik} + \mathbf{u}_{ik}{}'(\mathbf{p}_i^+ - \hat{\mathbf{R}}^+(\mathbf{q}_j^+))}{\sqrt{1 + \|\mathbf{q}_j^+\|^2}}$$

Now the numerator simplifies since, by Lemma 7-7, $\mathbf{p}_i^+ - \hat{\mathbf{R}}^+(\mathbf{q}_j^+) = \mathbf{p}_i - \hat{\mathbf{R}}(\mathbf{q}_j)$, and, since $\mathbf{q}_j = \hat{M}(\mathbf{p}_i)$, $\hat{\mathbf{R}}(\mathbf{q}_j) = \mathbf{p}_i + \hat{\epsilon}_i$, giving

$$d_{ik} + \mathbf{u}_{ik}{}'(\mathbf{p}_i^+ - \hat{\mathbf{R}}^+(\mathbf{q}_j^+)) \;=\; d_{ik} + \mathbf{u}_{ik}{}'(\mathbf{p}_i - \hat{\mathbf{R}}(\mathbf{q}_j))$$

$$=\; d_{ik} + \mathbf{u}_{ik}{}'(\mathbf{p}_i - (\mathbf{p}_i + \hat{\epsilon}_i)) \;=\; d_{ik} - \mathbf{u}_{ik}{}'\hat{\epsilon}_i$$

— but this expression measures the non-negative distance from $\hat{\epsilon}_i$ to the side of $\mathbf{p}_i$'s noise polygon specified by $< \mathbf{u}_{ik}, d_{ik} >$. Let us call this distance $\hat{c}_{ik}$.

We can bound the denominator from above:

$$\sqrt{1 + \|\mathbf{q}_j^+\|^2} \;\leqslant\; 1 + \|\mathbf{q}_j^+\|$$

$$=\; 1 + \|\hat{\mathbf{R}}^{-1}(\mathbf{p}_i^+ + \hat{\epsilon}_i)\| \;=\; 1 + \frac{1}{\hat{r}_s}\|\mathbf{p}_i^+ + \hat{\epsilon}_i\|$$

$$\leqslant\; 1 + \frac{\|\mathbf{p}_i^+\| + \|\hat{\epsilon}_i\|}{\hat{r}_s} \;\leqslant\; \frac{\hat{r}_s + \rho_{max} + \epsilon}{\hat{r}_s}$$

Combining these, we have, for noise constraint $< \mathbf{u}_{ik}, d_{ik} >$, a lower bound

$$\frac{\hat{c}_{ik}\,\hat{r}_s}{\rho_{max} + \epsilon + \hat{r}_s} \tag{8-1}$$

on the closest approach of the corresponding registration constraint hyperplane to $\hat{\mathbf{R}}^+$.

Since we want to bound from below the quantity c_i^+, the closest approach to $\hat{\mathbf{R}}^+$ among all l_{max} constraints, we must choose, for use in (8-1), the value $\min_{k=1,...,lmax}\{\hat{c}_{ik}\}$ — but this minimum is simply the closest approach of $\hat{\epsilon}_i$ to the sides of the noise polygon for $\mathbf{p}_i$, which we have called $\hat{c}_i$. ∎

8.3. Expected Number of Contractions

Theorem 8-1. For random P, Q, generated using fixed κ, ϵ, $\dot{\mathbf{R}}$, and $\ddot{M}$, after matched-centroid and farthest-first preprocessing, the expected number of ellipsoid contractions required to prove $\hat{M}$ feasible, counting *only* along the search path to $\hat{M}$, is $O(\log n)$.

Proof. Let random variable C_n be the number of contractions required to prove $\hat{M}$ feasible, counting only along the search path from $\hat{M}_1$ to $\hat{M}_n = \hat{M}$. As we have seen,

$$C_n \leq \log_\sigma \left[\frac{Vol(\mathbf{E}_1)}{Vol(\mathbf{F}_n)} \right].$$

where $\mathbf{E}_1$ is an initial ellipsoid for 1-matching $\hat{M}_1$ and $\mathbf{F}_n$ is the final feasible region determined by $\hat{M}_n$. Thus $C_n \leq \log_\sigma(Vol(\mathbf{E}_1)) - \log_\sigma(Vol(\mathbf{F}_n))$, and

$$E[C_n] \leq E[\log_\sigma(Vol(\mathbf{E}_1))] - E[\log_\sigma(Vol(\mathbf{F}_n))] \tag{8-2}$$

We need an upper bound on $E[\log_\sigma(Vol(\mathbf{E}_1))]$. Lemma 8-1 provides an upper bound on $Vol(\mathbf{E}_1)$:

$$Vol(\mathbf{E}_1) \leq \frac{32\pi^2}{3} \frac{\epsilon^4 \hat{r}_s^2}{(\rho_{max} - 2\epsilon)^2}, \tag{8-3}$$

so,

$$E[\log_\sigma(Vol(\mathbf{E}_1))] \;\leqslant\; \log_\sigma\left[\frac{32\,\pi^2\,\epsilon^4\,\hat{r}_s^2}{3}\right] \;-\; 2\,E[\log_\sigma(\rho_{max}-2\,\epsilon)] \quad (8\text{-}4)$$

We know from Lemma 7-10 that

$$E[\rho_{max}] \;\geqslant\; \left[\frac{2\,n\,\sqrt{n}}{n+\frac{1}{2}} - \sqrt{2}\right]\frac{\epsilon}{\sqrt{\kappa}}$$

and thus increases without bound as $n \rightarrow \infty$, as κ and ϵ remain constant. Therefore $E[\log_\sigma(\rho_{max}-2\,\epsilon)]$ must go positive for all sufficiently large n, and its contribution cannot worsen the upper bound of (8-4) asymptotically, and may be dropped, giving (for sufficiently large n):

$$E[\log_\sigma(Vol(\mathbf{E}_1))] \;\leqslant\; \log_\sigma\left[\frac{32\,\pi^2\,\epsilon^4\,\hat{r}_s^2}{3}\right] \;=\; O(1) \quad (8\text{-}5)$$

since only n is considered to vary. (It is interesting to note that, if $\hat{\mathbf{R}}$ were considered to vary, we would have $O(\log\hat{r}_s)$; in fact, throughout the following analysis, there are latent dependencies on the scale of the generating registration $\hat{\mathbf{R}}$ — but not on its rotation or translation — however, we will not explore these here.)

Examining now the second term of (8-2), we need a lower bound on $E[\log_\sigma(Vol(\mathbf{F}_n))]$. We will construct a 4-D sphere $\mathbf{S}_n$, of radius r_n, which is entirely enclosed within $\mathbf{F}_n$. By Lemma 8-2, for each $i = 1,...,n$, the matched pair $\hat{M}(\mathbf{p}_i) = \mathbf{q}_j$ determines a set of l_{max} registration constraint hyperplanes which approach $\hat{\mathbf{R}}^+$ no more closely than

$$c_i^+ \;\geqslant\; \frac{\hat{c}_i\,\hat{r}_s}{\rho_{max}+\epsilon+\hat{r}_s} \quad,$$

where $\hat{c}_i$ is the closest approach of noise vector $\hat{\epsilon}_i$ to the sides of the noise polygon for $\mathbf{p}_i$. If we identify r_n with $\min_{i=1,...,n}\{c_i^+\}$, then a sphere centered at $\hat{\mathbf{R}}^+$ of radius r_n is contained entirely within all registration constraint hyperplanes for $\hat{M}_n$, and so is contained within $\mathbf{F}_n$. Thus $Vol(\mathbf{F}_n) \;\geqslant\; Vol(\mathbf{S}_n) = \dfrac{\pi^2\,r_n^4}{6}$, and so

$$E[\,\log_\sigma(\textit{Vol}(\mathbf{F}_n))\,] \;\geqslant\; 4\,E[\,\log_\sigma r_n\,] \;+\; \log_\sigma \frac{\pi^2}{6} \quad . \tag{8-6}$$

Call $\hat{c}_{min} \equiv \min\limits_{i\,=\,1,\ldots,n} \{\hat{c}_i\}$, then

$$r_n \;\geqslant\; \frac{\hat{c}_{min}\,\hat{r}_s}{\rho_{max} + \epsilon + \hat{r}_s} \quad,$$

and so

$$E[\,\log_\sigma r_n\,] \;\geqslant\; E[\,\log_\sigma \hat{c}_{min}\,] \;-\; E[\,\log_\sigma(\rho_{max} + \epsilon + \hat{r}_s)\,] \;+\; \log_\sigma \hat{r}_s \tag{8-7}$$

Taking the second term on the right side of (8-7) first, we can use the fact that $log\,(\cdot)$ is concave to apply Jensen's inequality for an upper bound:

$$E[\,\log_\sigma(\rho_{max} + \epsilon + \hat{r}_s)\,] \;\leqslant\; \log_\sigma(\,E[\rho_{max}] + \epsilon + \hat{r}_s\,)$$

$$\leqslant\; \log_\sigma \left[\; \left[\frac{2n\sqrt{n}}{n + \frac{1}{2}} + \sqrt{2}\,\right] \frac{\epsilon}{\sqrt{\kappa}} + \epsilon + \hat{r}_s \right]$$

$$\leqslant\; \log_\sigma \left[\; \left[\frac{2\sqrt{n} + \sqrt{2}}{\sqrt{\kappa}} + 1\right] \epsilon + \hat{r}_s \right]$$

$$=\; O(\log n) \quad . \tag{8-8}$$

Now, returning to (8-7) and taking the first term on the right side, we need a lower bound on $E[\,\log_\sigma \hat{c}_{min}\,] = \log_\sigma e\; E[\,\ln \hat{c}_{min}\,]$ (note: $\log_\sigma e > 0$). By Lemma 7-6, the probability density function of random variable $\hat{C}_{min} = \hat{c}_{min}$ is

$$f\hat{c}_{min}(c) \;=\; \frac{2n}{H^{2n}}\,(H - c)^{2n-1}$$

where $H = \epsilon\cos\dfrac{\pi}{l_{max}}$, and $c \in [0, H]$. Thus we may compute

$$E[\,\ln \hat{c}_{min}\,] \;=\; \int_0^H \ln c\; f\hat{c}_{min}(c)\; dc$$

$$= \frac{2n}{H^{2n}} \int_0^H \ln c \; (H-c)^{2n-1} \; dc$$

(changing variable to $t \equiv c/H$, so that $t \in [0,1]$)

$$= 2n \int_0^1 (\ln t + \ln H) \; (1-t)^{2n-1} \; dt$$

$$= 2n \int_0^1 \ln t \; (1-t)^{2n-1} \; dt \; + \; 2n \ln H \int_0^1 (1-t)^{2n-1} \; dt \qquad (8\text{-}9)$$

Now, $\int_0^1 (1-t)^{2n-1} \; dt = 1/2n$, so the right term becomes simply $\ln H$. The

left term, changing variables with $s = 1-t$, is equal to

$$L = 2n \int_0^1 s^{2n-1} \ln(1-s) \; ds$$

The definite integral has a closed-form solution [31], which gives:

$$L = 2n \left[\frac{1}{2n} \left(s^{2n} - 1 \right) \ln(1-s) \; - \; \frac{1}{2n} \sum_{r=1}^{2n} \frac{s^r}{r} \right]_{s=0}^{s=1}$$

$$= - \sum_{r=1}^{2n} \frac{1}{r} \; = \; -\left(\ln(2n) + \gamma + O\left(\frac{1}{n}\right) \right)$$

Substituting this in turn into (8-9), and taking the negative (making for a more natural use of $O(.)$-notation), we have

$$-E[\log_\sigma \hat{c}_{min}] \; = \; -(\log_\sigma e) \; E[\ln \hat{c}_{min}]$$

$$= \; \log_\sigma e \; (\ln(2n) + \gamma + O\left(\frac{1}{n}\right) - \ln H) \; = \; O(\log n) \quad .$$

Substituting this and (8-8) into (8-7), again taking the negative, we have

$$-E[\log_\sigma r_n] \; \leqslant \; O(\log n) + O(\log n) - \log_\sigma \hat{r}_s \; = \; O(\log n) \quad .$$

Substituting this into the negative of (8-6) gives

$$- E[\log_\sigma(Vol(\mathbf{F}_n))] \quad \leqslant \quad 4\,O(\log n) - \log_\sigma \frac{\pi^2}{6} \quad = \quad O(\log n) \quad .$$

Finally, substituting this and (8-5) into (8-2) gives

$$E[C_n] \quad \leqslant \quad O(1) + O(\log n) \quad = \quad O(\log n) \quad \blacksquare$$

Corollary 8-3. For random P, Q, generated using fixed κ, ϵ, $\hat{\mathbf{R}}$, and $\hat{M}$, after matched-centroid and farthest-first preprocessing, the expected runtime required to prove $\hat{M}$ feasible, counting *only* along the search path to $\hat{M}$, is $O(n \log n)$.

Proof. To perform the matched-centroid and farthest-first preprocessing takes $O(n)$ time (Sections 7.5.1 & 7.5.2). To compute the initial ellipsoid $\mathbf{E}_1$ for $\hat{M}_1$ takes $O(1)$ time (see Corollary 7-2). The total number of matchings examined, only along the search path to $\hat{M}$, is $O(n)$. The expected number of contractions to prove $\hat{M}$ feasible is, by Theorem 8-2, $O(\log n)$, for fixed $\hat{\mathbf{R}}$. The cost of a contraction for a k-matching is $O(k)$ (Section 4.3.2). Thus the expected runtime required to perform contractions is $O(n \log n)$. The expected total runtime is therefore $O(n \log n)$. $\blacksquare$

8.4. Summary

This analysis of costs holds along only a single, special path in the search tree. As far as we know, the fact that this path is guaranteed to be one of the longest may not imply that its cost dominates those of other paths. We have not yet found good methods of attacking other paths. An important obstacle is our lack of understanding of the behavior of a sequence of contracting ellipsoids when the final outcome is infeasibility.

Later, in Chapter 10, we report empirical results from Monte Carlo trials which indicate that the expected costs incurred along other paths are at least as low as those proved in this special case.

CHAPTER 9.

Expected Size of Search Tree

We now investigate the expected total number of feasible matchings examined by the search algorithm. It is possible analytically to identify, at each node in the search tree, which successor matchings are "good candidates" for feasibility. This analysis can be used to show that for any fixed scale of noise, there is some confusion factor κ for which the expected number of feasible matchings is linear in n. Further, the analysis gives a fast test that can be used to declare "bad candidates" infeasible.

9.1. Predictive Matching

Suppose k instance points have been matched successfully, giving the current k-matching M_k and a current ellipsoid $\mathbf{E}_k$, whose center is a currently feasible registration $\mathbf{R}_k$. The next model point to be matched is $\mathbf{p}_{k+1}$. There are $n - k$ instance points remaining that are candidates for a match. How many of these, on average, are feasible? We attack this by asking related question, how many are "good candidates" for feasibility?

We can use the current ellipsoid $\mathbf{E}_k$ to "probe" the set of instance points for good candidates (see Figure 9-1). The feasible registration $\mathbf{R}_k$ can be used to mis-register $\mathbf{p}_{k+1}$, giving $\mathbf{R}_k^{-1}(\mathbf{p}_{k+1})$; clearly, if an instance point happened to coincide with this point, it would be a feasible match for $\mathbf{p}_{k+1}$. Now suppose registration $\mathbf{R}_k + \delta\mathbf{R}$ is feasible, then, similarly, $(\mathbf{R}_k+\delta\mathbf{R})^{-1}(\mathbf{p}_{k+1})$ would be a feasible match for $\mathbf{p}_{k+1}$. If, in addition, $\mathbf{p}_{k+1} + \epsilon_{k+1}$ falls inside the noise polygon for $\mathbf{p}_{k+1}$, then $(\mathbf{R}_k+\delta\mathbf{R})^{-1}(\mathbf{p}_{k+1} + \epsilon_{k+1})$ would also be a feasible match for $\mathbf{p}_{k+1}$.

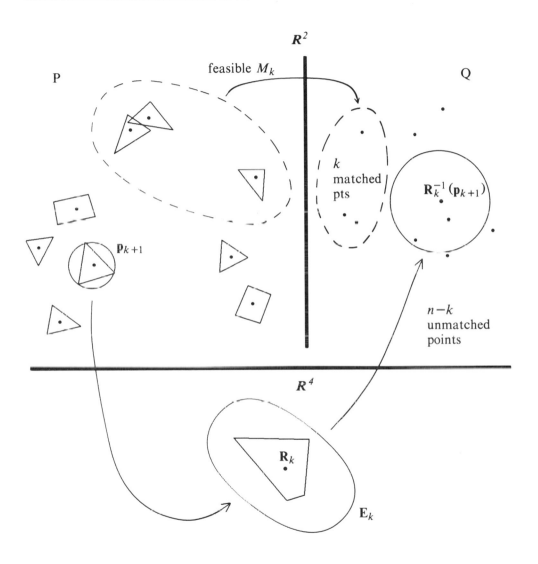

Figure 9 - 1. Predictive matching, using a probe circle.

We now show how to isolate analytically the effects of model noise and registration variations on the location of candidate instance points.

Lemma 9-1. For any model point $\mathbf{p}$, noise vector $\boldsymbol{\epsilon}$, registration $\tilde{\mathbf{R}}$, and incremental registration $\delta\mathbf{R}$, the point $\mathbf{q} = (\tilde{\mathbf{R}} + \delta\mathbf{R})^{-1}(\mathbf{p} + \boldsymbol{\epsilon})$ can be written as $\tilde{\mathbf{q}} + \delta\mathbf{q}$, where

$$\tilde{\mathbf{q}} = \tilde{\mathbf{R}}^{-1}(\mathbf{p}) \quad \text{and} \quad \delta\mathbf{q} = \frac{\boldsymbol{\epsilon} - \delta\mathbf{R}(\tilde{\mathbf{q}})}{\tilde{r}_{12} + \delta r_{12}} .$$

Proof. By direct calculation:

$$\delta\mathbf{q} = \mathbf{q} - \tilde{\mathbf{q}} = (\tilde{\mathbf{R}} + \delta\mathbf{R})^{-1}(\mathbf{p} + \boldsymbol{\epsilon}) - \tilde{\mathbf{q}}$$

$$= \frac{(\mathbf{p} + \boldsymbol{\epsilon}) - (\tilde{\mathbf{r}}_{xy} + \delta\mathbf{r}_{xy})}{\tilde{r}_{12} + \delta r_{12}} - \tilde{\mathbf{q}}$$

$$= \frac{\mathbf{p} + \boldsymbol{\epsilon} - \tilde{\mathbf{r}}_{xy} - \delta\mathbf{r}_{xy} - \tilde{r}_{12}\tilde{\mathbf{q}} - \delta r_{12}\tilde{\mathbf{q}}}{\tilde{r}_{12} + \delta r_{12}}$$

Now, $\tilde{r}_{12}\tilde{\mathbf{q}} = \tilde{r}_{12}\tilde{\mathbf{R}}^{-1}(\mathbf{p}) = \mathbf{p} - \tilde{\mathbf{r}}_{xy}$, so

$$\delta\mathbf{q} = \frac{\boldsymbol{\epsilon} - (\delta r_{12}\tilde{\mathbf{q}} + \delta\mathbf{r}_{xy})}{\tilde{r}_{12} + \delta r_{12}} = \frac{\boldsymbol{\epsilon} - \delta\mathbf{R}(\tilde{\mathbf{q}})}{\tilde{r}_{12} + \delta r_{12}} \quad \blacksquare$$

We now apply this to the predictive matching problem, expressing model noise and registration variations as the effect of prior matching of at least two points.

Theorem 9-1. For any model P and instance Q, any k-matching M, $k \geqslant 2$, any two distinct matched points $\mathbf{q}_a = M(\mathbf{p}_a)$ and $\mathbf{q}_b = M(\mathbf{p}_b)$, any unmatched model point $\mathbf{p}_c$, any invertible registration $\mathbf{R}$, and any instance point $\mathbf{q}$, it is possible to write $\mathbf{q}$ as $\tilde{\mathbf{q}}_c + \delta\mathbf{q}_c$, where

$$\tilde{\mathbf{q}}_c = \bar{\mathbf{q}} + \frac{\Delta\mathbf{q}}{\Delta\mathbf{p}}(\mathbf{p}_c - \bar{\mathbf{p}})$$

$$\text{and} \qquad \delta\mathbf{q}_c \;=\; \frac{\Delta\mathbf{q}}{\Delta\mathbf{p}} \frac{(\epsilon_c - \bar{\epsilon})\Delta\mathbf{p} + (\mathbf{p}_c - \bar{\mathbf{p}})\Delta\epsilon}{\Delta\mathbf{p} + \Delta\epsilon}$$

and where: $\bar{\mathbf{p}} \equiv (\mathbf{p}_a + \mathbf{p}_b)/2$, $\Delta\mathbf{p} \equiv \mathbf{p}_b - \mathbf{p}_a$, and $\bar{\mathbf{q}}$ and $\Delta\mathbf{q}$ are defined analogously; $\bar{\epsilon}$ and $\Delta\epsilon$ are defined, as above, using $\epsilon_a \equiv R(\mathbf{q}_a) - \mathbf{p}_a$, $\epsilon_b \equiv R(\mathbf{q}_b) - \mathbf{p}_b$; and, finally, $\epsilon_c \equiv R(\mathbf{q}) - \mathbf{p}_c$.

Proof. Apply Theorem 7-1 to write $\mathbf{R}$ as $\tilde{\mathbf{R}} + \delta\mathbf{R}$, where

$$\tilde{\mathbf{R}} \;=\; \begin{bmatrix} \bar{\mathbf{p}} - \dfrac{\Delta\mathbf{p}}{\Delta\mathbf{q}}\bar{\mathbf{q}} \\[2ex] \dfrac{\Delta\mathbf{p}}{\Delta\mathbf{q}} \end{bmatrix} \qquad \text{and} \qquad \delta\mathbf{R} \;=\; \begin{bmatrix} \bar{\epsilon} - \dfrac{\Delta\epsilon}{\Delta\mathbf{q}}\bar{\mathbf{q}} \\[2ex] \dfrac{\Delta\epsilon}{\Delta\mathbf{q}} \end{bmatrix} \quad .$$

Then, apply Lemma 9-1, identifying its $\mathbf{p}$ with $\mathbf{p}_c$, ϵ with ϵ_c, $\tilde{\mathbf{R}}$ with $\tilde{\mathbf{R}}$, and $\delta\mathbf{R}$ with $\delta\mathbf{R}$. First we show that the $\mathbf{q}$ of this theorem is the same as the $\mathbf{q}$ of the lemma:

$$(\tilde{\mathbf{R}} + \delta\mathbf{R})^{-1}(\mathbf{p}_c + \epsilon_c) \;=\; (\tilde{\mathbf{R}} + \delta\mathbf{R})^{-1}(R(\mathbf{q})) \;=\; R^{-1}(R(\mathbf{q})) \;=\; \mathbf{q} \quad .$$

We may now use the Lemma to write $\mathbf{q}$ as $\tilde{\mathbf{q}}_c + \delta\mathbf{q}_c$, where

$$\tilde{\mathbf{q}}_c \;=\; \tilde{\mathbf{R}}^{-1}(\mathbf{p}_c) \qquad \text{and} \qquad \delta\mathbf{q}_c \;=\; \frac{\epsilon_c - \delta R(\tilde{\mathbf{q}}_c)}{\tilde{\mathbf{r}}_{12} + \delta\mathbf{r}_{12}} \quad .$$

Now,

$$\tilde{\mathbf{R}}^{-1}(\mathbf{p}_c) \;=\; \frac{\mathbf{p}_c - (\bar{\mathbf{p}} - \dfrac{\Delta\mathbf{p}}{\Delta\mathbf{q}}\bar{\mathbf{q}})}{\dfrac{\Delta\mathbf{p}}{\Delta\mathbf{q}}} \;=\; \bar{\mathbf{q}} + \frac{\Delta\mathbf{q}}{\Delta\mathbf{p}}(\mathbf{p}_c - \bar{\mathbf{p}}) \quad .$$

Also,

$$\frac{\epsilon_c - \delta R(\tilde{\mathbf{q}}_c)}{\tilde{\mathbf{r}}_{12} + \delta\mathbf{r}_{12}} \;=\; \frac{\epsilon_c - \delta R(\bar{\mathbf{q}} + \dfrac{\Delta\mathbf{q}}{\Delta\mathbf{p}}(\mathbf{p}_c - \bar{\mathbf{p}}))}{\dfrac{\Delta\mathbf{p}}{\Delta\mathbf{q}} + \dfrac{\Delta\epsilon}{\Delta\mathbf{q}}}$$

$$= \frac{\Delta q}{\Delta p + \Delta \epsilon} \left[\epsilon_c - \left[\frac{\Delta \epsilon}{\Delta q} (\bar{q} + \frac{\Delta q}{\Delta p} (p_c - \bar{p})) + (\bar{\epsilon} - \frac{\Delta \epsilon}{\Delta q} \bar{q}) \right] \right]$$

$$= \frac{\Delta q}{\Delta p + \Delta \epsilon} \left[\epsilon_c - \frac{\Delta \epsilon}{\Delta q} \bar{q} - \frac{\Delta \epsilon}{\Delta p} (p_c - \bar{p}) - \bar{\epsilon} + \frac{\Delta \epsilon}{\Delta q} \bar{q} \right]$$

$$= \frac{\Delta q}{\Delta p} \frac{(\epsilon_c - \bar{\epsilon}) \Delta p + (p_c - \bar{p}) \Delta \epsilon}{\Delta p + \Delta \epsilon} \quad \blacksquare$$

Corollary 9-1. For random P and Q generated using ϵ, any feasible k-matching M, $k \geqslant 2$, any two distinct matched points $q_a = M(p_a)$ and $q_b = M(p_b)$, and any unmatched model point p_c, there exists a fixed point $\tilde{q}_c$ located so that every instance point q that can be feasibly matched to p_c can be written $\tilde{q}_c + \delta q_c$, and δq_c is bounded as follows:

$$\| \delta q_c \| \leqslant \frac{\| \Delta q \|}{\| \Delta p \| - 2 \epsilon} \left[1 + \frac{\| p_c - \bar{p} \|}{\| \Delta p \|} \right] 2 \epsilon \quad .$$

Proof. Identify $\tilde{q}_c$ and δq_c with the variables of the same names in Theorem 9-1. Thus,

$$\| \delta q_c \| \leqslant \frac{\| \Delta q \|}{\| \Delta p + \Delta \epsilon \|} \left[\| \epsilon_c \| + \| \bar{\epsilon} \| + \| \Delta \epsilon \| \frac{\| p_c - \bar{p} \|}{\| \Delta p \|} \right]$$

Let $M\prime$ be the $(k+1)$-matching that extends M to include $q = M\prime(p_c)$. For the Corollary to hold, $M\prime$ must be feasible. Every registration **R** which is feasible for $M\prime$ must bound from above by ϵ the magnitude of the noise vectors ϵ_a, ϵ_b, and ϵ_c, as defined in Theorem 9-1. This, in turn, implies that $\| \bar{\epsilon} \| \leqslant \epsilon$, $\| \Delta \epsilon \| \leqslant 2\epsilon$, and $\| \epsilon_c \| \leqslant \epsilon$. Thus,

$$\| \delta q_c \| \leqslant \frac{\| \Delta q \|}{\| \Delta p \| - 2 \epsilon} \left[\epsilon + \epsilon + \frac{2 \epsilon \| p_c - \bar{p} \|}{\| \Delta p \|} \right]$$

$$\leqslant \quad \frac{\|\Delta q\|}{\|\Delta p\| - 2\epsilon} \left[1 + \frac{\|p_c - \bar{p}\|}{\|\Delta p\|} \right] 2\epsilon \quad \blacksquare$$

9.2. Expected Number of Feasible Matchings

We can now derive upper bounds on $E[F(n)]$, the expected total number of feasible matchings encountered while searching for successful matchings of random P and Q. First, we place an upper bound on the fraction of unmatched instance points that are "good candidates" for matching, in the sense that they lie within a probe circle guaranteed to contain all instance points that can be feasibly matched.

Corollary 9-2. For random P and Q generated using ϵ and $\hat{R}$, after matched-centroid and farthest-first preprocessing, any feasible k-matching M, $k \geqslant 1$, and any unmatched model point p, all instance points which can be feasibly matched to p lie within a circle of radius no more than $\left[\dfrac{\rho_{max} + 2\epsilon}{\rho_{max} - 2\epsilon} \right] \dfrac{5\epsilon}{\hat{r}_s}$.

Proof. The center of the desired circle is $\tilde{q}_c$, and the radius is $\|\delta q_c\|$, of Corollary 9-1. Applying matched-centroid and farthest-first preprocessing to P and Q of Corollary 9-1 reduces the size of the matching necessary from $k \geqslant 2$ to $k \geqslant 1$, and we can choose to identify the p_a and p_b of Corollary 9-1 with p_0^+ and p_1^+, q_a and q_b with q_0^+ and $q_a^+ = M(p_1^+)$, and $\bar{p}_c$ with p. Then $\|\Delta p\| = \rho_{max}$, $\|\bar{p}\| = \rho_{max}/2$, and $\|\Delta q\| - \|q_a^+\| \leqslant (\rho_{max} + 2\epsilon)/\hat{r}_s$. Substituting into the result for Corollary 9-1,

$$\|\delta q_c\| \quad \leqslant \quad \frac{\rho_{max} + 2\epsilon}{\hat{r}_s\,(\rho_{max} - 2\epsilon)} \left[1 + \frac{\|p\|}{\rho_{max}} + \frac{\frac{\rho_{max}}{2}}{\rho_{max}} \right] 2\epsilon$$

Now, notice that $\|p\| \leqslant \rho_{max}$ by farthest-first preprocessing. Thus,

$$\|\delta q_c\| \quad \leqslant \quad \frac{\rho_{max} + 2\epsilon}{\rho_{max} - 2\epsilon} \left[1 + 1 + \frac{1}{2} \right] \frac{2\epsilon}{\hat{r}_s}$$

$$= \frac{\rho_{max} + 2\epsilon}{\rho_{max} - 2\epsilon} \frac{5\epsilon}{\hat{r}_s} \qquad \blacksquare$$

Note that this result does not depend on the location of **p**. This makes possible a strong result.

Lemma 9-2. For random P and Q generated using *fixed* ϵ and κ, after matched-centroid and farthest-first preprocessing, any feasible k-matching M, $k \geqslant 1$, and any unmatched model point **p**, the expected fraction of unmatched instance points that are good candidates to match **p** is $O(1/n)$ — more sharply, for any κ and $\alpha > 0$, there is some n_α such that for all $n > n_\alpha$, the expected fraction is no more than $\frac{(9+\alpha)\kappa}{n}$.

Proof. The probe center and radius given by Corollary 9-2 were computed using only one original instance point, $q_a^+ = M(p_1^+)$, along with the origin $q_0^+ = (0,0)$. Thus the probe center was chosen independently of the set of unmatched instance points. We can therefore apply Lemma 7-3, to conclude that the expected fraction of unmatched instance points falling within the probe circle is at most

$$\left(\frac{\left[\left[\frac{\rho_{max} + 2\epsilon}{\rho_{max} - 2\epsilon} \right] \frac{5\epsilon}{\hat{r}_s} \right] \hat{r}_s + \epsilon}{\rho} \right)^2$$

$$= \left[5 \left[\frac{\rho_{max} + 2\epsilon}{\rho_{max} - 2\epsilon} \right] + 1 \right]^2 \left[\frac{\epsilon}{\rho} \right]^2$$

Now, for random P and Q generated using ϵ and κ, we know from Section 7.2 that $\rho = 2\epsilon\sqrt{n/\kappa}$, so $\left[\frac{\epsilon}{\rho} \right]^2 = \frac{\kappa}{4n}$. Thus, the expected fraction of good candidates among unmatched instance points is at most

$$\left[\frac{5}{2} \left(\frac{\rho_{max} + 2\epsilon}{\rho_{max} - 2\epsilon} \right) + \frac{1}{2} \right]^2 \frac{\kappa}{n} \quad .$$

Now we recollect, from Lemma 7-10, that for any fixed ϵ and κ, as $n \to \infty$, $E[\rho_{max}]$ increases without bound. Thus the expected value of the expression $\left(\dfrac{\rho_{max} + 2\epsilon}{\rho_{max} - 2\epsilon} \right)$ will asymptotically approach 1 from above, for any fixed ϵ and κ, and

$$\left[\frac{5}{2} \left(\frac{\rho_{max} + 2\epsilon}{\rho_{max} - 2\epsilon} \right) + \frac{1}{2} \right]^2$$

will asymptotically approach 9 from above. Thus the expected fraction of unmatched instance points that are good candidates to match **p** will asymptotically approach $\dfrac{9\kappa}{n}$ from above, for any fixed ϵ and κ.

We can conclude that the expected fraction is $O(1/n)$. Also, we can make the sharper observation that for any κ and $\alpha > 0$, there is some n_α such that for all $n > n_\alpha$, the expected fraction is no more than $\dfrac{(9+\alpha)\kappa}{n}$. ∎

Given a feasible $(k-1)$-matching ($k \geq 2$), the probability that any particular successor k-matching is also feasible is no more than $\dfrac{(9+\alpha)\kappa}{n}$ asymptotically, for any $\alpha > 0$ and $n > n_\alpha$. Let $\kappa_\alpha \equiv (9+\alpha)\kappa$, and for the rest of this section assume $n > n_\alpha$.

Let us assume that there are exactly m total feasible matchings to be found by an exhaustive search of the tree — that is, $f(n,n) = m$. Suppose we know $E[f(n,k-1)]$ for some $k \geq 2$. Then $E[f(n,k)]$ is at most m (for the feasible predecessors of the m total feasible matchings), plus the fraction $\dfrac{\kappa_\alpha}{n}$ of the $n-(k-1)$ successors of each feasible $(k-1)$-matching:

$$E[f(n,k)] \leqslant m + \frac{\kappa_\alpha}{n} (n - (k-1)) E[f(n,k-1)] .$$

Suppose $E[f(n,j)]$ is known, $0 \leqslant j < k-1$, then by induction $E[f(n,k)] \leqslant$

$$m \left[1 + \sum_{l=j+1}^{k-1} \left[\kappa_\alpha^{k-l} \prod_{i=l}^{k-1} \frac{n-i}{n} \right] \right] + \left[\kappa_\alpha^{k-j} \prod_{i=j}^{k-1} \frac{n-i}{n} \right] E[f(n,j)]$$

Now, of course, for any x such that $1 \leqslant x \leqslant k-1 < n$, $\displaystyle\prod_{i=x}^{k-1} \frac{n-i}{n} \leqslant 1$, so,

$$E[f(n,k)] \leqslant m \left[1 + \sum_{l=j+1}^{k-1} \kappa_\alpha^{k-l} \right] + \kappa_\alpha^{k-j} E[f(n,j)] .$$

We can now see an opportunity to characterize "moderate" noise precisely: if κ_α were less than 1, the geometric series $\displaystyle\sum_{l=j+1}^{k-1} \kappa_\alpha^{k-l}$ converges for increasing n and k. (This is not to say that $E[f(n,k)]$ will *diverge* for $\kappa_\alpha \geqslant 1$ — these bounds may be loose.)

Theorem 9-2. For any *fixed* $\epsilon > 0$, there exists a *confusion threshhold* $\kappa_0 > 0$, such that for any random P and Q generated using ϵ and $\kappa < \kappa_0$, under matched-centroid and farthest-first strategies, the expected total number of feasible matchings examined to identify m successful matchings is $O(mn)$.

Proof. In the terms of Lemma 9-2, choose any $\alpha > 0$, then let $\kappa_0 = 1/(9+\alpha)$. Thus when $\kappa < \kappa_0$, $\kappa_\alpha = (9+\alpha)\kappa < 1$, for $n > n_\alpha$. Now, we can sum the series:

$$\sum_{l=j+1}^{k-1} \kappa_\alpha^{k-l} = \sum_{l=1}^{k-j-1} \kappa_\alpha^l = \frac{\kappa_\alpha (1 - \kappa_\alpha^{k-j-1})}{1 - \kappa_\alpha} \leqslant \frac{\kappa_\alpha}{1 - \kappa_\alpha} ,$$

yielding the result,

$$E[f(n,k)] \leqslant m \left[1 + \frac{\kappa_\alpha}{1 - \kappa_\alpha} \right] + \kappa_\alpha^{k-j} E[f(n,j)]$$

$$= \frac{m}{1 - \kappa_\alpha} + \kappa_\alpha^{k-j} \, E[f(n,j)] \quad .$$

Now we can compute the expected total number of feasible k-matchings, $k \geqslant j$, given $E[f(n,j)]$:

$$E[\sum_{k=j}^{n} f(n,k)] \quad = \quad \sum_{k=j}^{n} E[f(n,k)]$$

$$\leqslant \quad \sum_{k=j}^{n} \left[\frac{m}{1 - \kappa_\alpha} + \kappa_\alpha^{k-j} \, E[f(n,j)] \right]$$

$$= \quad \frac{m(n-j+1)}{1 - \kappa_\alpha} + \left[\sum_{k=j}^{n} \kappa_\alpha^{k-j} \right] E[f(n,j)]$$

$$= \quad \frac{m(n-j+1)}{1 - \kappa_\alpha} + \frac{1 - \kappa_\alpha^{n-j+1}}{1 - \kappa_u} \, E[f(n,j)]$$

$$\leqslant \quad \frac{m(n-j+1)}{1 - \kappa_\alpha} + \frac{1}{1 - \kappa_\alpha} \, E[f(n,j)]$$

$$= \quad \frac{1}{1 - \kappa_\alpha} \left[m(n-j+1) + E[f(n,j)] \right] \quad .$$

These results hold for $j \geqslant 1$, by Lemma 9-2, and we know that $f(n,1) \leqslant n$, so let us pick $j = 1$, and we have:

$$E[F(n)] \quad = \quad \sum_{k=1}^{n} E[f(n,j)] \quad = \quad O(mn+n) \quad = \quad O(n) \quad \blacksquare$$

The "confusion threshhold" value κ_0 between guaranteed linear and possibly exponential growth of feasible matchings would appear, from this analysis, to be $= 1/(9+\alpha)$, for $\alpha > 0$, and so to be no more than $1/9 \approx 0.1$. However, the bounds used in the proof are loose. In Chapter 10, we will show that, for κ up to at least 1.0, and n up to at least 36, the average number of successful matchings $(E[m])$ is less than two, and the average number of feasible matchings encountered appears linear in n. Thus the result of Theorem 9-2 appears to hold for a scale of noise often occurring in practice.

9.3. Locating Good Candidates

The "probe circles" developed earlier, aside from their value in proving asymptotic bounds on feasible matchings, also promise a means for efficiently selecting good candidate points. The preceding discussion gives us a means for constructing, for each node in the search tree at depth $k \geqslant 2$, a "probe circle" outside of which no instance point can be a feasible match for $\mathbf{p}_{k+1}$.

Let $\tilde{\mathbf{q}}$ be the center, and $\| \delta\mathbf{q} \|$ the radius of a probe circle. Then if

$$\| \mathbf{q} - \tilde{\mathbf{q}} \| \;>\; \| \delta\mathbf{q} \| \quad ,$$

$\mathbf{q}$ cannot be feasible. This test can be performed in 6 floating-point operations: two multiplies, two subtracts, an addition, and a compare. Following the convention that will be used in Chapter 10, we will count only multiplies, divides, and squareroots (the adds, subtracts, and compares are proportional to these). Thus the cost of this test is simply two floating-point multiplies.

This contrasts strongly with the cost to test feasibility using the ellipsoid method. First, l_i ($\geqslant 3$) noise constraints must be transformed into registration constraints, at a cost of 6 multiplies per constraint. Then, each registration constraint must be compared to the ellipsoid center, for 4 multiplies each. At least one constraint must fail to be satisfied, and have to be compared with the volume of the ellipsoid, requiring 24 multiplies. This gives at least 54 so far. Some number of contractions may be required before infeasibility is finally proven, at a cost of dozens of multiplies per contraction. Finally, all l_i constraints must be found to exclude the final ellipsoid, for an additional cost of at least 48 multiplies. Thus, even ignoring the possibility of contractions, 102 multiplies are required. This is a factor of 50 more costly than the test using the probe circle.

We will see in the next chapter that these "bad candidate" tests are so much faster than the main engine of the Ellipsoid algorithm that their cost is negligible even for large patterns.

CHAPTER 10.

Monte Carlo Trials

To judge our algorithm's performance in practice, we have run Monte Carlo trials, generating random models, noise, and instances as described in Chapter 7. For patterns of up to 36 points, under "moderate" noise ($\kappa < 1.0$), the average total cost (in floating-point operations) of running the Soviet ellipsoid algorithm is apparently linear in n. The average total number of "good candidates", including all feasible matchings, is apparently $O(n)$. The average total number of "bad candidates" examined, however, is $\Theta(n^2)$. Thus the average total runtime required to explore the full tree, reporting all successful matchings, appears to be $O(n^2)$. However, we project that for patterns of less than 100 points, runtime will appear effectively linear, since non-linear terms contribute less than 5% of the total cost.

10.1. Design of Trials

The pseudorandom number generator used was developed by Swain & Swain [32].

Without loss of generality, we fixed at 10.0 units the radius ρ within which the model points are chosen. The scale of noise was controlled, as discussed in Section 6.2, by choice of an upper bound κ on the expected number of model points "confusable" with a given random model point. The upper bound on noise ϵ was then computed using $\epsilon = \frac{\rho}{2} \sqrt{\kappa/n}$.

Three values of κ were investigated, covering at least the range likely to be encountered using practical feature extractors (see Figure 10-1).

$\kappa = 1.0$ "high" noise, illustrated in Figure 10-1 (a); this level of noise yields on average at least one spurious matching, for most values of n, and so is

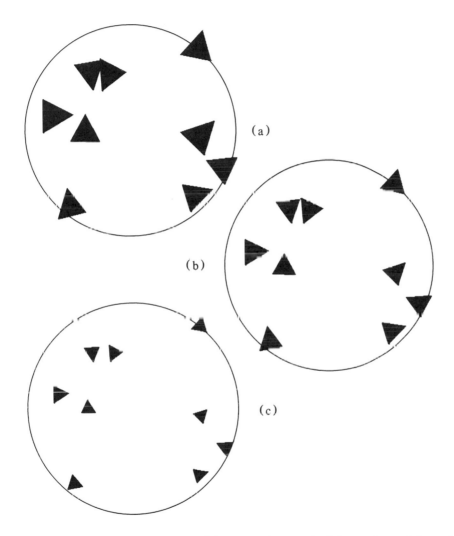

Figure 10 - 1.   Degrees of noise: (a) "high" ($\kappa = 1.0$); (b) "moderate" ($\kappa = 0.5$); and (c) "low" ($\kappa = 0.2$).

perhaps atypically high for practical purposes.

$\kappa = 0.5$ "moderate" noise, illustrated in Figure 10-1 (b); this level of noise seems reasonable to expect from a practical feature extractor; good results here should predict good results in practice.

$\kappa = 0.2$ "low" noise, illustrated in Figure 10-1 (c); this level of noise seems too small to reflect experience with practical feature extractors.

Noise polygons were equilateral triangles of maximum radius ϵ, rotated at an angles chosen uniformly and independently in $[0, 2\pi]$. Noisy model points were chosen uniformly and independently within the area of these triangles.

Mis-registration functions $\hat{\mathbf{R}}^{-1}$ were also chosen randomly, as follows. (This policy challenges the algorithm more than the expected-case theorems we have presented, all of which assumed $\hat{\mathbf{R}}$ was fixed; we will see that, in spite of this, the random trial results are consistent with the theorems.) A translation vector $\hat{\mathbf{r}}_{xy}$ was chosen uniformly within a circle of radius 5.0 units about the origin. A rotation angle $\hat{r}_\theta$ was chosen uniformly in $[0, 2\pi]$. A scale factor $\hat{r}_s$ was permitted to vary within the bounds $[1/3, 3]$, with $\log \hat{r}_s$ being chosen uniformly within the interval $[\log(1/3), \log(3)]$. Using these, $\hat{\mathbf{r}}_{12}$ was computed. The resulting mis-registration function $\hat{\mathbf{R}}^{-1}$ was applied to the noisy model points, giving the points of the random instance.

Finally, an n-permutation $\hat{M}$ was chosen, uniformly among all n-permutations, and used to shuffle the order of the instance points, giving the random instance.

For each value of κ, and for each value of $n = 6, 9, 12, ..., 36$, we ran 100 random trials.

The matched-centroid and farthest-first strategies described in Section 6.2 were used to compute prior constraints on registrations, leading to some pruning of matchings of size 1. For each matching of size 2, an initial ellipsoid was computed as described in Section 7.8.

10.2. Cost of Testing

The mean total number of ellipsoid contractions, for $\kappa = 0.5$, is shown in Figure 10-2. It appears linear in the range of n shown. The multiplicative constant of growth, for $\kappa = 0.5$, is about 18 contractions per model point.

Based on this, we could conservatively project that the mean cost of testing would be $O(n^2)$, since each contraction testing a k-matching costs $O(k)$ arithmetic operations. However, when we plot the total testing effort (floating-point

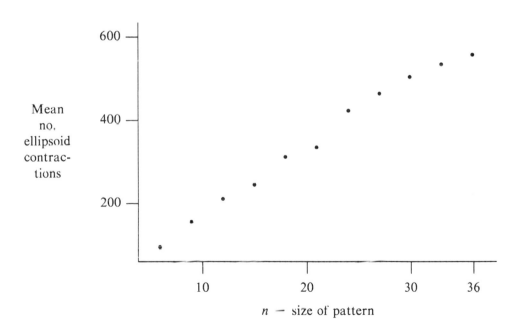

Figure 10-2.   Cost of testing: mean total number of ellipsoid contractions ($\kappa = 0.5$, 100 random trials per datum).

multiplies and divides, Figure 10-3), we observe a better result: it too appears linear in n. The multiplicative constant of growth, for $\kappa = 0.5$, is about 4500 floating-point multiplies per model point. This suggests that the great majority of contractions occur at the higher levels of the tree.

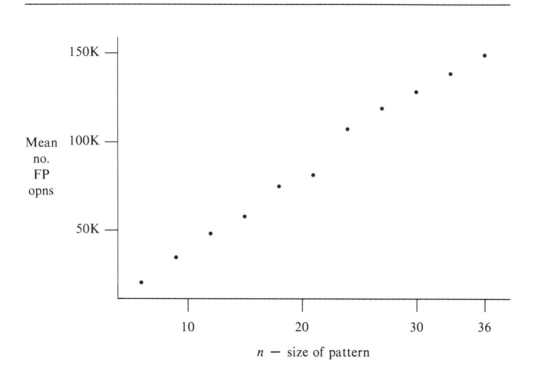

Figure 10 - 3.   Cost of testing: mean total number of floating-point operations ($\kappa = 0.5$, 100 random trials per datum).

10.3. Size of the Search Tree

Using lexicographic search order, in which all $(n-k)$ successors of a feasible k-matching are routinely tested, the total number of matchings tested is, as shown in Section 4.2.1, $\Omega(n^2)$, and this was clear during trials (see Figure 10-4a): by plotting the square-root of these values (in Figure 10-4b) and checking for linearity, the growth rate can be seen to be nearly exactly quadratic.

Predictive matching was used to count the number of "good candidate" matchings. The probe circles were computed using the ellipsoid of the ancestral 2-matching, rather than the current ellipsoid, as a matter of programming convenience. Even though this meant using a generally larger ellipsoid, the results were good: we observed linear growth for κ as high as 1.0 (see Figure 10-5). This is a higher value of κ than is likely to occur in practice, as we have seen. It is also better behavior than suggested by the analysis of Chapter 9, where it was proven that linear growth would occur for $\kappa \leqslant 0.1$.

The multiplicative factor of growth, for $\kappa = 0.5$, is about 9 good candidates per model point.

10.4. Non-linear Costs

Testing "bad" candidates is the only remaining non-linear cost. In Chapter 9 it was shown that the cost of testing a bad candidate was only two floating-point multiplies. The average number of good candidates is linear in n, and the cost of testing them is (empirically) about 4500 floating-point multiplies per model point. Thus we see that, in practice, for $n < 100$ points, the share of the cost contributed by testing bad candidates is less than 5%:

$$\frac{2 \cdot 100^2}{4500 \cdot 100 + 2 \cdot 100^2} \approx 0.04 \quad .$$

Thus a user can expect that for $n < 100$, the average runtime of the algorithm on random patterns under moderate noise is "practically" linear in n.

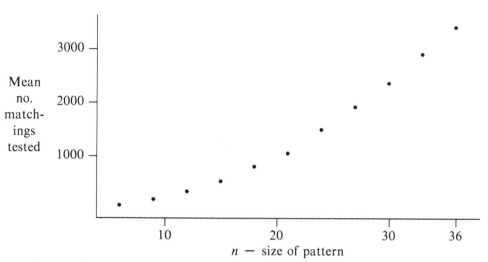

Figure 10-4a.   Mean size of search tree ($\kappa = 0.5$, 100 trials per datum).

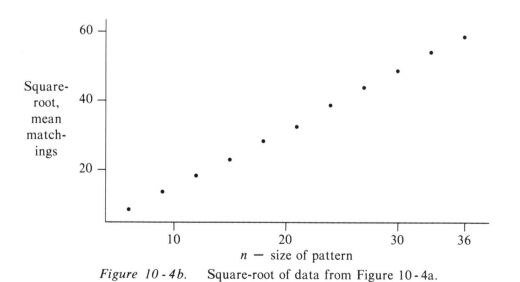

Figure 10-4b.   Square-root of data from Figure 10-4a.

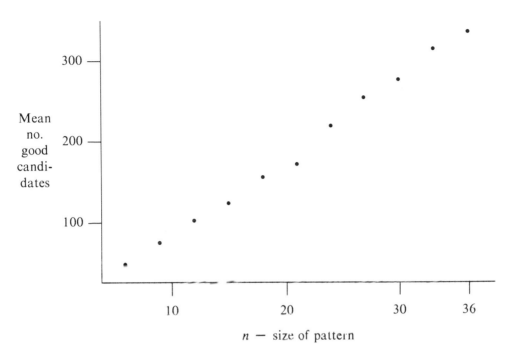

Figure 10-5. Mean total number of "good candidates," including all feasible matchings ($\kappa = 0.5$, 100 random trials per datum).

CHAPTER 11.

Conclusions

Finally, we will point out some interesting unfinished business and extensions, and summarize the principal results.

1.1. Miscellaneous Extensions

We have deliberately impoverished pattern features, considering only their location, to prove the advantage of exploiting geometrical constraints. In practice, features are often richer in properties. It is straightforward within our method to exploit geometrical properties other than location, such as size and orientation of features. Each additional property can be used to further constrain the set of feasible registrations, and faster pruning will result.

An important special case occurs where the elementary features are straight-line segments. Expected runtimes comparable to those we have proven for point features could be achieved for line features, *without* the assumption that no features are missing or spurious. In the case of point features, that assumption was needed principally to provide a bounded feasible region for 1-matchings, so that some 2-matchings are pruned, and an n^2 cost at the outset is avoided. But, for lines, matching *one* pair of features is sufficient to bound the feasible region.

Clearly, the method can be extended to arbitrary affine "registrations" acting on higher-dimensional spaces. An important special case is arbitrary translation, rotation, and scaling in three-space: it may be possible efficiently to match features of solid bodies, given a range map of the scene.

Motion analysis is another natural application. The knowledge that from frame to frame the registration could not have changed by much would provide tight registration constraints at the outset of matching each frame.

Our use of depth-first pruned search also invites the heuristic use of non-geometric feature properties, such as semantic labels and order relations, to guide or further prune the generation of partial matchings. In this way, many previous matching methods can coexist with ours.

11.1. Spurious & Missing Points

The analysis and Monte Carlo results presented apply if there are no spurious or missing instance points.

If only a few spurious points occur, and are clustered at random among the good instance points, the prior registration constraints will be only slightly looser, and the algorithm should degrade gracefully. Matching will continue as usual until n instance points are matched, but of course extra successful matchings may be found. The selection of "good candidate" instance points using probe circles should be a particularly valuable pruning method when the number of randomly-located spurious points is large.

If it is known that exactly m instance points are missing, but none are spurious, then a variation on our method may be effective. This is simply to "turn around" the matching method. Rather than fixing a comparison order on the model points, and then pairing instance points to them systematically, fix an order on the instance points instead, and then pair the model points to them. No successful matchings will be overlooked, and the pruning method will work as before, with matching succeeding when $n - m$ pairs are found feasible. We believe that the matched-centroid and farthest-first strategies can be applied as before, and, under a suitable random model, will degrade slowly as the number of missing points increases.

If *both* missing and spurious instance points are expected, then we have not found any way to relieve the combinatorial explosion that results. Suppose it is known that no more than s instance points may be spurious, and no more than m missing. One method that ensures that no successful matching is overlooked is to add s "wild-card" points to the model (which by *fiat* will be immediately-feasible matches for any instance point), and similarly add m wild-card points to the instance pattern. Wild-card matches are declared feasible immediately, by the algorithm responsible for generating matchings, without requiring expensive artifices such as huge noise polygons — in fact, without requiring any increased work by the ellipsoid machinery. Then the problem is to match two sets of $n + s$ points until a successful $n + s$ matching is found. This could in the worst case lead to $s! m!$ extra matchings being tested.

11.2. Summary of Results

The use of well-understood ideas from linear programming theory provides a rigorous and general framework for exploiting location of feature points in planar pattern matching.

Representing location error distributions as convex polygons allows good approximation of many types of worst-case noise found in practice, and copes with variations in types of noise among feature points within the same pattern. Such noise constraints can be provided automatically by a variety of feature extraction methods.

It has been difficult to analyze asymptotic worst-case size of the search tree, except for highly regular patterns in the limiting case of zero noise. For a large class of such patterns, the worst-case number of feasible matchings found by the algorithm is shown to be $O(n^2 \log n)$. Using the assumption that there are no spurious or missing points, we have found ways to place prior constraints on registrations, which dramatically reduce asymptotic growth for all but essentially circular patterns.

For a class of random patterns, under the assumption of no spurious or missing points, we have shown that, along special long paths in the search tree, the expected cost of feasibility-testing by the Soviet ellipsoid algorithm is only $O(n \log n)$. Also, we have established that, for average patterns, there is a scale of non-zero noise for which the expected total number of feasible matchings examined to find m successful matchings is $O(\, m\,n\,)$.

Random trials indicate that this scale of noise includes most cases likely to arise in practice, and so we term it "moderate" noise. Average runtimes under moderate noise were observed to be $O(n^2)$. For patterns with fewer than 100 points, we project that average runtimes will appear effectively linear in n, since the contribution of non-linear growth terms amounts to less than 5%.

APPENDIX

As promised in Chapter 6, we will exhibit a 2-dimensional pattern for which every 2-possible k-matching can be extended to a feasible k-matching.

Consider the pattern formed by tiling the plane with equilateral triangles, where the vertices of the triangles are the pattern points. We will define a "triangular lattice" coordinate system so that the pattern points are exactly the points having integer lattice coordinates. The lattice axes, *right* and *up*, meet at an angle of 60° (see Figure A-1). Let $[r,u]$ denote a point referenced to this coordinate system, and let $\begin{bmatrix} x \\ y \end{bmatrix}$ denote a point in the Cartesian plane. For any real r and u, define

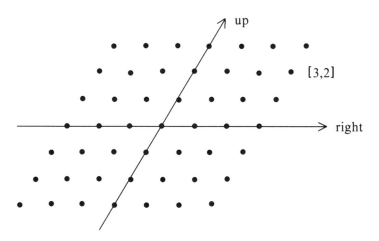

Figure A-1.   Triangular lattice and coordinate system.

$$[r,u] \equiv \begin{pmatrix} r + u \cos 60° \\ u \sin 60° \end{pmatrix}$$

It is easy to see that the set $\{\ [u,v]\ |\ u,\ v\ \textit{integers}\ \}$ forms a pattern based on a triangular tiling. Let $p_1 = [0,0]$ and number the points in order of nondecreasing distance from p_1 -- this produces a class of patterns that satisfies the three properties of Section 6.1.

Lemma A-1. For any two pattern points, there is a third pattern point completing an equilateral triangle.

Proof: Given two pattern points p_a and p_b, there exist integers r_a, u_a, r_b, u_b such that $p_a = [r_a, u_a]$ and $p_b = [r_b, u_b]$. Now compute the point

$$p_c = p_a + rot_{-60°}(p_b - p_a)$$

which completes one of the two equilateral triangles with base p_a - p_b. Having computed p_c, we will show that its lattice coordinates are integral.

$$p_c = \begin{pmatrix} r_a + u_a \cos 60° \\ u_a \sin 60° \end{pmatrix}$$

$$+ \begin{bmatrix} \cos 60° & \sin 60° \\ -\sin 60° & \cos 60° \end{bmatrix} \left\{ \begin{pmatrix} r_b + u_b \cos 60° \\ u_b \sin 60° \end{pmatrix} - \begin{pmatrix} r_a + u_a \cos 60° \\ u_a \sin 60° \end{pmatrix} \right\}$$

$$= \begin{pmatrix} r_a + u_a/2 \\ u_a \sqrt{3}/2 \end{pmatrix} + \begin{bmatrix} 1/2 & \sqrt{3}/2 \\ -\sqrt{3}/2 & 1/2 \end{bmatrix} \begin{pmatrix} (r_b - r_a) + (u_b - u_a)/2 \\ (u_b - u_a)\sqrt{3}/2 \end{pmatrix}$$

$$= \begin{pmatrix} r_a + u_a/2 \\ u_a \sqrt{3}/2 \end{pmatrix} + \begin{pmatrix} \dfrac{1}{2}((r_b - r_a) - (u_b - u_a)) \\ \dfrac{\sqrt{3}}{2}((r_b - r_a) + (u_b - u_a)) \end{pmatrix}$$

$$= \begin{pmatrix} \dfrac{1}{2}((r_b + r_a) - (u_b - 2u_a)) \\ \dfrac{\sqrt{3}}{2}((r_b - r_a) + u_b) \end{pmatrix}$$

Now, we notice that

$$
[\, r_a + u_a - u_b, \quad u_b + r_b - r_a \,] \;=\; \begin{pmatrix} r_a + u_a - u_b + \dfrac{1}{2}\,(\, u_b + r_b - r_a \,) \\[2ex] \dfrac{\sqrt{3}}{2}\,(\, u_b + r_b - r_a \,) \end{pmatrix}
$$

$$
=\; \begin{pmatrix} \dfrac{1}{2}\,(\, (r_b + r_a) - (u_b - 2\,u_a)\,) \\[2ex] \dfrac{\sqrt{3}}{2}\,(\, (r_b - r_a) + u_b \,) \end{pmatrix}
$$

Therefore,

$$
p_c \;=\; [\, r_a + u_a - u_b, \quad u_b + r_b - r_a \,]
$$

and its lattice coordinates are integers. Thus p_c is a pattern point. ▮

Theorem A-1. For the triangular lattice, any 2-possible k-matching can be extended to a feasible k-matching.

Proof sketch. A 2-possible k-matching determines a registration superimposing the points p_1 and p_2 of P_k onto some p_a and p_b of P_n. Since P_n is a subset of the triangular lattice, p_a and p_b are on the lattice.

Now P_k is a subset of the lattice, and points forming equilateral triangles before registration still do after registration. Therefore in the registered image of P_k, every point either completes a triangle whose base is p_a - p_b, or inductively can be located by completing a series of triangles, starting with the base p_a - p_b. Since p_1 and p_2 are on the (unregistered) lattice, by the lemma and simple induction, every point in P_k is also on the lattice.

Finally, by the definition of 2-possible matchings, p_a and p_b have been chosen so that every point of the registered image of P_k falls within the bounds of P_n. By definition, every lattice point within the bounds of P_n is a member of P_n. Therefore, every point of the registered image of P_k coincides with some point of P_n. This gives the necessary extension of the 2-possible matching to a full k-matching of zero error, and this full matching is thus feasible. ▮

REFERENCES

[1] D. Nitzan, G. Agin, R. Bolles, G. Gleason, J. Hill, D. McGhie, R. Prajoux, A. Sword, & W. Park, *Machine Intelligence Research Applied to Industrial Automation,* SRI International, Menlo Park, California, August 1979.

[2] W. A. Perkins, "A Model-Based Vision System for Industrial Parts," *IEEE Trans. Computers*, vol. C-27 no. 2, pp. 126-143, February 1978.

[3] T. Pavlidis, *Structural Pattern Recognition.* New York: Springer-Verlag, 1977. Chs. 6-9.

[4] K. S. Fu, *Syntactic Methods in Pattern Recognition.* New York: Academic Press, 1974.

[5] L. Baumert, D. Lieberman, & H. Rumsey, "K[h]achlan's Ellipsoidal Algorithm," Working paper No. 622, Communication Research Division, Institute for Defense Analyses, Princeton, NJ, February 1981.

[6] U. Grenander, *Pattern Analysis.* New York: Springer-Verlag, 1978, pp. 269-273.

[7] D. Lavine, B. A. Lambird, & L. N. Kanal, "Recognition of Spatial Point Patterns," *Proc. Conf. Pattern Recognition & Image Processing*, Dallas, Texas, pp. 49-53, August 1981.

[8] D. Kahl, A. Rosenfeld, & A. Danker, "Some Experiments in Point Pattern Matching," *IEEE Trans. Sys. Man. Cyber.*, vol 10, pp. 105-116, 1980.

[9] G. B. Dantzig, *Linear Programming and Extensions.* Princeton, NJ: Princeton University Press, 1963.

[10] T. Pavlidis & S. L. Horowitz, "Segmentation of Plane Curves," *IEEE Trans. Computers*, C-23 No. 8, pp. 860-870, August 1974.

[11] J. C. Simon, A. Checroun, & C. Roche, "A Method of Comparing Two Patterns Independent of Possible Transformations and Small Distortions", *Pattern Recognition*, No. *4*, pp. 73-81, 1972.

[12] C. Zahn, "An Algorithm for Noisy Template Matching", *Proc. IFIP 74*, pp. 727-732, 1974.

[13] R. A. Seidl, "A Theory of Structure and Encoding of Visual Patterns with Applications to Character Recognition", Ph.D. Dissertation, Univ. Newcastle (Australia), 1974.

[14] K. Price & R. Reddy, "Matching Segments of Images", *IEEE Trans. PAMI*, vol. PAMI-1 no. 1, pp. 110-116, January 1979.

[15] H. G. Barrow, J. M. Tenenbaum, R. C. Bolles, & H. C. Wolf, "Parametric Correspondence and Chamfer Matching: Two New Techniques for Image Matching", *Proc. Intl Joint Conf. Artificial Intelligence*, pp. 659-663, 1977.

[16] S. Ranade & A. Rosenfeld, "Pattern Matching by Relaxation", *Pattern Recognition*, no. *12*, pp. 269-275, 1980.

[17] H. Tropf, "Analysis-by-Synthesis Search for Semantic Segmentation Applied to Workpiece Recognition", *5th Intl Conf. Pattern Recognition*, Miami Beach, Florida, pp. 241-244, December 1980.

[18] C. H. Papadimitriou & K. Steiglitz, *Combinatorial Optimization: Algorithms and Complexity*. Englewood Cliffs, NJ: Prentice Hall, 1982.

[19] E. M. Reinhold, J. Nievergelt, & N. Deo, *Combinatorial Algorithms: Theory and Practice*. Englewood Cliffs, NJ: Prentice Hall, 1977, pp. 161-164.

[20] R. C. Bolles & R. Cain, "Recognizing and Locating Partially Visible Objects: the Local Feature Focus Method," Tech. Note 262, SRI International, Inc., Menlo Park, CA, March 1982.

[21] J. Hill, "Dimensional Measurements from Quantized Images," *Machine Intelligence Research Applied to Industrial Automation,* (10th report), SRI International, Menlo Park, CA, March 1982.

[22] P. Billingsley, *Probability and Measure*. New York: John Wiley & Sons, 1979, pp. 219-233.

[23] D. H. Ballard, "Generalizing the Hough Transform to Detect Arbitrary Shapes," *Pattern Recognition,* vol. 13 no. 2, pp. 111-122, 1981.

[24] D. B. Gennery, "A Feature-Based Scene Matcher," *Proc. 7th Intl Joint Conf. Artificial Intelligence*, Vancouver, B.C., Canada, pp. 667-673, August 1981.

[25] K. Lieberherr, Princeton University, private communication, April 1981.

[26] E. H. McCall, "Performance Results of the Simplex Algorithm for a set of Real-World Linear Programming Models," *Communications of the ACM*, vol. *25*, No. 3, pp. 207-212, March 1983.

[27] H. Solomon, *Geometric Probability*, SIAM (Philadelphia, 1978).

[28] A. Rosenfeld, "Rapporteur for Sensing Systems," *Proceedings, Workshop on the Research Needed to Advance the State of Knowledge in Robotics*, Newport, RI, pp. 198-205. 15-17 April, 1980.

[29] J. G. Ecker & M. Kupferschmid, "A Computational Comparison of Several Nonlinear Programming Algorithms," Report OR&S-82-2, Rensselaer Polytechnic Institute, Troy, NY, 25 July 1982.

[30] A. Rosenfeld & A. C. Kak, *Digital Picture Processing*, Section 8.3, Academic Press, New York, 1976.

[31] *Handbook of Chemistry and Physics (52nd Edition)*, Chemical Rubber Company, p. A-151, Equation 501, 1971.

[32] Swain & Swain, "A Uniform Random Number Generator that is Reproducible, Hardware-Independent, and Fast," MIT 1-31-80, Massachusetts Institute of Technology, Cambridge, MASS, 1980.

[33] A. V. Aho, J. E. Hopcroft, & J. D. Ullman, *The Design and Analysis of Computer Algorithms,* Chapter 1, Addison-Wesley, Reading, 1974.

[34] E. M. McCall, "Performance Results of the Simplex Algorithm for a Set of Real-World Linear Programming Models," *Communications of the ACM*, *25*, No. 3, pp. 207-212, March 1982.

[35] N. Megiddo, "Towards a Genuinely Polynomial Algorithm for Linear Programming," Discussion paper No. 493, Center for Mathematical Studies in Economics and Management Science, Northwestern University, Evanston, Illinois, August, 1981.

[36] N. Megiddo, "Linear-time Algorithms for Linear Programming in R^1 and Related Problems," Department of Statistics, Tel Aviv University, January 1982.

[37] *Jahresbericht der Deutschen Math. Vereinigung*, vol. 43, p. 114, 1934.

[38] L. S. Davis, "Shape Matching Using Relaxation Techniques," *IEEE Transactions on Pattern Analysis and Machine Intelligence*, Vol. PAMI-1, No. 1, pp. 60-72, January 1979.

[39] B. Chazelle, "The Polygon Containment Problem," *Advances in Computing Research*, vol. 1, JAI Press, Inc, Greenwich, CONN, pp. 1-33, 1983.

INDEX